DISCARD

LIBRARIES

LIBRARIES

ADDRESSES AND ESSAYS

BY JOHN COTTON DANA

Essay Index Reprint Series

BOOKS FOR LIBRARIES PRESS
FREEPORT, NEW YORK

First Published 1916
Reprinted in this Series 1966, 1969

STANDARD BOOK NUMBER:
8369-1329-9

LIBRARY OF CONGRESS CATALOG CARD NUMBER:
67-22088

PRINTED IN THE UNITED STATES OF AMERICA

PREFACE

The first of the addresses here printed was delivered in 1896, the last in 1915, and they thus cover twenty years of my experience as librarian in three cities. They are reprinted, at my own suggestion, in the hope that they contain somewhat of interest and value, especially to the younger members of our calling, and that they will attract a few general readers.

For twenty-five years I have devoted myself quite persistently to promoting the habits of reading, of using libraries and of book buying. This work has been very fascinating. One of its most attractive features has been its constant change in method, in scope and in material. I have seen that fundamental thing in library management, the relation of the tax-payer to his public library, change from the method of rigid supervision in 1894, in which year only four of a national gathering of about 125 librarians voted for the open shelf, to that of to-day, when almost every library of note eagerly invites its visitors to handle its books. In these same twenty-five years librarians have given up the age-limit method which kept children out of libraries, for the attraction method which lures them in. In 1890 libraries quite definitely pursued repose; to-day they seek results. In 1890 a citizen who wished to take home a library book was inspected for maturity, integrity and sweet reasonableness, and was guaranteed to possess these attributes by a fellow citizen of good repute for the same, before his wish was granted. To-day an entry in a city directory is ample evidence that one pos-

v

PREFACE

sesses proper book-borrowing qualities; and a library's
eagerness to serve often supplies a directory's defi-
ciencies.

Under the influence of Mr. Carnegie's gifts,
whose wealth is probably as great a surprise to him
as his generosity is to the world, expensive library
buildings have multiplied rapidly since 1890. Many
of these seem to have been ingeniously planned to
furnish a minimum of inconvenient space at a maximum of cost; still, they have increased enormously
popular interest in libraries and in appropriations
of public funds therefor. Library workers have
also increased greatly in number, as is indicated
by the national association's membership, which was
290 in 1890 and is over 3,000 to-day.

The first school of library science was opened
in 1887 by Mr. Dewey, against the protests of many
worthy librarians who felt that the art of library
management did not lie within the field of education. To-day 10 library schools of good standing
have a total of 300 pupils, and minor schools and
training classes have many more.

In my quarter century of work I have seen libraries of 5,000 volumes and over increase from
about 1,200 to about 3,000, and the total volumes in
all our libraries increase from 26,600,000 to 75,000,000.
The census tells us that in the same twenty-five
years the money invested in printing and publishing plants of all kinds has grown from $195,387,000
to over $600,000,000, with a corresponding increase
in output. This increase in the output of the printing press is the thing which, perhaps above all other
factors, is bringing about a radical revolution in
library method. What I have already said may seem
to indicate that the changes in the art of library man-

PREFACE

agement of the past twenty-five years have been
sufficiently radical; and that the modern practice
of that art conforms to all the demands born of
changes in material and clientele. But I believe
I have shown in this book that in the art of librarianship,—the art of promoting the use of print to civil
ends,—the rising flood of print and that increase
of its use which is at once the immediate cause
of the flood and a result thereof, will soon compel
changes in practice more fundamental than any that
have gone before. Not many men of books, as one
may call librarians, have gone out into the world;
but their books have, and they must follow them.
For every craft, for every art, for every trade, for
every kind of business, for every profession, for every
social question, there now comes forth daily a
veritable army of printed things, greater than any
statistics save that of the capital invested in printing can do more than vaguely suggest. And it is
well to call this vast output of print an army and
not a flood, for it is irrepressibly militant. It compels attention; and it finds waiting a vast multitude
of readers, daily added to by our schools, which
surrenders gladly to its assaults. Certain qualities
of this innumerable host of printed pages, and an
inevitable increase in the use of printed pages by
all manner of men, demand, as I have said, changes
in the librarian's method, so radical as to compel in
him who would wisely adopt them a quite definite
change in his conception of his calling.

In this volume I have not attempted to say definitely how the librarian of the future will adapt
his practice to the new conditions. I have tried
only to make it quite clear that the wise librarian
will keep his mental manners plastic and his professional methods flexible. And perhaps here lies

PREFACE

my chiefest reason for thinking that it may prove
worth while to reprint these papers—that they
quite urgently insist that, after an enthusiasm born
of love of the calling, the one most essential attri-
bute of the librarian, if he would be forever helpful and
never an obstacle, is a profound belief that the end
is not yet, that new conditions arise daily and that
they can be wisely met only after a confession of
ignorance, a surrender of all doctrine and careful
and unprejudiced observations.

JOHN COTTON DANA

Newark, N. J., June 1, 1916

CONTENTS

CONTENTS

CONTENTS

xi

LIBRARIES

HEAR THE OTHER SIDE

President's Address to the American Library Association, Cleveland Conference, September, 1896

"Failures confessed are guide-posts to success; weaknesses discovered are no longer weaknesses."

I sometimes fear my enthusiasm for the free public library is born more of contagion than of conviction. Consider the thing in some of its more evident aspects.

Here is a building, perhaps erected to perpetuate a good man's memory, a monument and of use only as a monument; or constructed in accordance with the views of an architect whose ideas of beauty are crude and whose thought of utility is naught; ill-adapted to the purpose for which it is intended; poorly lighted, badly ventilated. In it are stored a few thousand volumes, including, of course, the best books of all times—which no one reads—and a generous percentage of fiction of the cheaper sort. To this place come in good proportion the idle and the lazy; also the people who cannot endure the burden of a thought, and who fancy they are improving their minds, while in fact they are simply letting cool waters from fountains of knowledge trickle through the sieves of an idle curiosity. The more persistent visitors are often men who either have failed in a career, or never had a career, or do not wish a career. Libraries all have their indolents, idlers and "boarders."

There is little that is inspiring, *per se*, in the sight of the men who gather in the newspaper reading room of any free public library. There is not much that is encouraging in a careful look at many

3

of those who are the more constant visitors to the shelves of the reference department. Who wear out our dictionaries, the students of language or the competitors in a word building contest? Of those who come to the delivery desk 60 to 80 per cent rarely concern themselves, as far as the library knows them, with anything but fiction, and in that field concern themselves generally only with the latest novel, which they wish because it is the latest. And of this 60 to 80 per cent, a large proportion—probably at least half—prefer to get, and generally do get, a novel of the poorer kind.

I am stating the case plainly. I share the librarian's enthusiasm; but that enthusiasm is sometimes to me, and I believe to many others, a cause for surprise. Has it not often come sharply home to every librarian—the hopelessness of the task we assume to set ourselves? The triviality of the great mass of the free public library's educational work? The discouraging nature of the field? The pettiness, the awful pettiness, of results?

Nor is this all. That we strive for great things and accomplish so little; that our output seems not commensurate with the size of the plant and the cost of its maintenance, this is by no means the only fact which may rightly sober our enthusiasms.

Fathers and mothers love their children and look after their happiness. The more they do this, the more they concern themselves that the human beings they have brought into the world be self-reliant, self-supporting people, knowing how to live in harmony with their fellows, and wishing so to live, the more civilized are they. Parental responsibility is something the sense of which has never been too acute. That I may rightly scorn and despise my neighbor if his children be not decent, attractive, civilized; that my neighbor may rightly consider himself disgraced if his offspring grow not up in the fear and admonition of the good citizen; these things are not yet commonly received. The native manners and the education of the American child are looked upon, not so much as the result of parentage and home training, as the good gift of God and the public school.

A strong sense of parental responsibility, this is a prime essential to the growth of knowledge and to the increase of social efficiency. And this feeling of obligation to train properly the souls of one's own creation; this sense that the parent can win public approval as a parent only when the result is an additional factor in the public's happiness and comfort; this rule of living would surely result, if rightly applied, in careful consideration of the child's education. But what have we done? We have turned the whole subject of education over to the community. We have made it depend very largely on the result of an annual election. We have let it slip gradually into the hands of those veritable and inevitable children of government—the politicians. The American parent is indifferent to the character of the education of his children. The interposition of the community in what should be his affairs has not only made him indifferent to those affairs, it has made others indifferent that he is so. He pays his taxes. If the schools are poor the fault is at the school-board's door, not his.

The free public library not only relieves the idle and incompetent and indifferent from the necessity —would he have books—of going to work to earn them; it not only checks the growth of the tendency of the private individual to collect a library of his

5

own, adapted to his own needs, and suiting his own tastes and those of his childen; it also tends to lead parents to become indifferent to the general reading of their children, just as the free public school may lead them to be indifferent to their formal education. Certainly, fathers and mothers whose children use public libraries seem to care very little what and how much their children read. They conceal their solicitude from librarian and assistants, if it exists. Yet, if a collection of books in a community is a good thing for the community—and we seem to think it is; and if it is a good thing particularly for the children of the community—and we seem to think it is, then it is a good thing, not in itself simply, not as an object of worship, not as an adequate excuse for the erection of a pleasing mortuary monument on the public street, but for its effect on young folks' manners and on young folks' brains. But to produce a maximum effect herein, to produce even a modest effect, the right books must be put into the right hand at the right time. Can public servants do this rightly unless the parents cooperate with them? But the public library is not an institution which the mother helps to support because she has come to believe in it; because it is her pleasure; because she can and does keep a watchful eye on its growth and its methods. It is part of the machinery of the state. She confides her children to its tender mercies in the same spirit with which her forbears confided in their king!

Furthermore, the essence of government is force. This essence remains whether the visible form be king or majority. It is open to question—I put it mildly —whether it is expedient to touch with the strong hand the impulse of a people to train with earnest

6

thought their young, or the impulse of a people to give light to their fellows. People wish, in the main, that their children be well taught. Without this wish a school system, public or private, would be impossible. This wish is the fundamental fact; that the system is public and tax-supported is the secondary fact; the result, not the cause. People wish also, in the main, to give their fellows and themselves the opportunity for self improvement. This wish is the fundamental fact at the bottom of the free, compulsorily supported public library. It is on these fundamental facts we should keep our eyes and our thoughts, not on the feature of compulsion.

We should work, then, such is my conclusion, for the extension of the public library from the starting point of human sympathy; from the universal desire for an increase of human happiness by an increase of knowledge of the conditions of human happiness; not from the starting-point of law, of compulsion, of enforcing on others our views of their duty.

I have said enough in this line. To the observant eye our libraries are not altogether halls of learning; they are also the haunts of the lazy. They do not always interest parents in their children; perhaps they lead parents to be indifferent to their children.

But really, librarians will say, all this is not our concern. We find ourselves here, they say, loving the companionship of books; desirous of extending the joys they can give to our fellows; embarked in public service, and active—none are more so; zealous —none are more so; honest—none are more so, in our work of making good use of books. Your modern librarian in his daily life is no disputatious economist, idly wavering, like the fabled donkey, between the loose hay of a crass individualism and the chopped feed of a perfectionist socialism. He is a worker. If there are things to be said which may add to the efficiency of his attempts to help his fellows to grow happier and wiser, let us hear them; and for this we have come together.

I have said these things, not with the wish to lessen the zeal of one of us in our chosen work. A moment's look at the case against us cannot anger us—that were childish; cannot discourage us—that were cowardly. It may lead us to look to the joints in our armor; it should lead us to renew our efforts. If the free public library movement be not absolutely and altogether a good thing, and he is a bold economist who vows that it is, how urgent is the call to us to make each our own library the corrective, as far as may be, of the possible harm of its existence. A collection of books gathered at public expense does not justify itself by the simple fact that it is. If a library be not a live educational institution it were better never established. It is ours to justify to the world the literary warehouse. A library is good only as the librarian makes it so.

Can we do more than we have done to justify our calling? Can we make ourselves of more importance in the world, of more positive value to the world? Our calling is dignified in our own eyes, it is true; but we are not greatly dignified in the eyes of our fellows. The public does not ask our opinions. We are, like the teachers, students; and we strive, like them, to keep abreast of the times, and to have opinions on vital topics formed after much reading and some thought. But save on more trivial questions, on questions touching usually only the recreative side of life, like those of literature commonly so called,

our opinions are not asked for. We are, to put it
bluntly, of very little weight in the community. We
are teachers; and who cares much for what the
teacher says?

I am not pausing now to note exceptions. We all
know our masters and our exemplars; and I shall not
pause to praise the men and women who have brought
us where we are; who have lifted librarianship, in the
estimation of the wise and good, to a profession, and
have made it comparatively an easy thing for you and
me to develop our libraries, if we can and will, into
all that they should be, and to become ourselves, as
librarians, men and women of weight and value in
the community.

I have said that your library is perhaps injuring
your community; that you are not of any importance
among your own people. And these, you tell me are
hard sayings. In truth they are. I am not here to
pass you any compliments. If for five minutes we
can divest ourselves of every last shred of our trap
pings of self-satisfaction, and arouse in ourselves for
a moment a keen sense of our sins of omission, of
things left undone or not well done, I shall be content,
and shall consider that we have wisely opened these
Cleveland sessions. I would wish to leave you, here
at the very beginning of our discussions, not, indeed
in the Slough of Despond, but climbing sturdily, and
well aware that you are climbing, the Hill Difficulty.
Others, I can assure you, will, long before our conference ends, lead us again, and that joyfully, to our
Delectable Mountains.

Pardon me, then, while I say over again a few of
the things that cannot be too often said.

Look first to your own personal growth. Get into

touch with the world. Let no one point to you as an instance of the narrowing effects of too much of books.

Be social. Impress yourself on your community; in a small way if not in a large. Be not superior and reserved. Remember that he who to the popular eye wears much the air of wisdom is never wise.

Speak out freely on matters of library management; and especially, in these days, on matters of library construction. In recent years millions of dollars have been spent on library buildings in this country, and we have not yet a half dozen in the land that do not disgrace us. If we have stood idly by and not made our opinions, our knowledge, our experience, felt by trustees and architects, then is ours the blame, and we are chief among the sufferers. Persuade architects and their associations, local and national, who ignore us because in our inconsequence they know they can, that they may wisely and without loss of dignity consult the professional librarian about the building he is to occupy. I say persuade them; I might better say compel them. To compel them will be easy when you have become of importance in the world. Even now it is not too soon to attempt to confer with them. You can at once make the beginning of friendly and helpful relations with the American Institute of Achitects. But you must ask, not demand.

Advertise the A. L. A. and what it stands for. Help to broaden its field. Support heartily measures which look to a greater degree of publicity for it. Interest your trustees in it. Interest your friends, and your patrons and constituents in it. Be ready and willing to do your share of the work, and there is no end of work that each year must be done to keep it properly alive and well in the public eye. Call the attention of your trustees to the difference between the efficient library, such as the A. L. A. advocates, and the dead-and-alive collection of books, still altogether too common. Consider the contrast between the possible public library and the public library that is. If the causes for that contrast lie at your door, face them frankly and bravely and strive to remove them.

Do not forget the Library Department of the National Educational Association, recently established. It gives you excuse, and it gives you cause to take an interest, more active even than heretofore, in the introduction of books and library methods into school work, and to concern yourselves more than ever before with the general reading of teachers and their pupils. Impress upon teachers the value to them of your library. Persuade them, if you can, that to do their best work they must know well and use freely the good books.

See that your local book and news men are heartily with you in the work of spreading knowledge of the right use of books and in encouraging ownership of books in your community. If you come in contact with the bookseller and the publisher of the great cities, do what you can to persuade them that to join in the work of this association of librarians is not only to benefit the community at large, but to help their own particular business as well.

Be not slow in giving hearty recognition to those who have, in the beginnings of library science, taken the first place and borne the burdens and made an easy way for us who follow. If, perhaps against some odds, a librarian, man or woman, is making an eminent success of some great city library, may you

not properly send him, once and again, a word which
shall signify that you, at least, are alive to the fact
of his good work and are yourself encouraged and
inspired thereby? Like words of approval you may
well extend to the good men, outside the profession
proper, who have given their time and energy, a labor
of love, to improve certain features of library work.

Interest in your work in your own community
your local book-lovers and book-collectors and book-
worms and private students and plodders and burn-
ers of the midnight oil. Get in touch with the teachers of literature in the colieges and schools of your
neighborhood. Expound to such, and to the general
reader as well, whenever you properly can, the difficulties and the possibilities of your calling, your con-
quests in classification and cataloging, and your
advances in bibliography and indexing, and the progress in recent years of general library economy.
Remember that all these things can be even better
done in a small community, in the village library of a
few hundred volumes, than in the large library of the
great city.

Note the women's clubs, art associations, historical societies, scientific societies. Do not forget the
private schools. In the small town you can gain
without difficulty the good-will of the local newspaper. You can often assist the editor in his work,
and lead him to help you in return. The clergymen
in your town certainly care somewhat for the reading
of their young people, and will cooperate with you
in any intelligent effort to increase it and improve it.
The Sunday-school libraries of your neighborhood are
open to your suggestions, if you approach them properly. And the Y. M. C. and the Y. W. C. associations
will gladly take from you advice and assistance in

the management of their reading-rooms and their libraries.

None are so poor that they cannot give to others; and few libraries are so small that they cannot spare books and magazines enough to make a little library which may be sent out into a still smaller community and there do good service.

Do the business men and the business women, the active people, those who feed us and clothe us and transport us, those who have brought about in the last few decades the great increase in creature comforts for every one, do these business people take an active interest in your library? Do they care for you or for your opinion? If not, is it their fault? Is it that they are gross and dull and material and worldly; or is it that you, the wise librarian, know not yet how to bring your educational forces to bear on the life that now is? Our work is but begun so long as we are not in close touch with the man of affairs.

Remember that as you in your town, or in your city, widen the sphere of your influence, grow to be a person of worth and dignity in the community, you thereby add so much to the dignity and to the effectiveness of the whole profession. If in a city or town near you there is a library which, in its general arrangement is not what it should be, which is but a dusty pile of printed pages or but a roosting-place for a flock of cheap novels, yours is in part the fault, and you are largely the loser. When a dweller in that town, one unacquainted with library affairs— and most are such—hears you alluded to as a "librarian," he thinks of you as a person akin to the bibliothecal pagan who fails to manage the library of his own town, the only library he knows by which he can measure your work. He is a "librarian";

you are a "librarian." We wear the livery of our co-workers as well as our own.

Keep these thoughts in mind and you will see how essential it is, would our profession reach the standing we wish it to reach, would we make it everywhere an honor to wear our name, that every smallest library be an effective educational machine, and that every humblest librarian be an active, enthusiastic, intelligent worker.

See that your library is interesting to the people of the community, the people who own it, the people who maintain it. Deny your people nothing which the book-shop grants them. Make your library at least as attractive as the most attractive retail store in the community. Open your eyes to the cheapness of books at the present day, and to the unimportance, even to the small library, of the loss of an occasional volume; and open them also to the necessity of getting your constituency in actual contact with the books themselves.

Remember always that taxation is compulsion, that taxation is government; that government, among present-day human creatures, is politics; that the end of an institution may not justify its means; that a free public library may be other than a helpful thing. See to it, therefore, the more carefully that your own public library at least is rationally administered, and promotes public helpfulness.

THE PUBLIC AND ITS PUBLIC LIBRARY

Popular Science Monthly, June, 1897

The opponents of the system of free, tax-supported public schools never have been answered. That they are wrong in their position is not proved, as so many seem to think, by a simple reference to the great growth and seeming success of the free public-school system and its attendant free public library system in this country. An institution may thrive, may apparently fulfill the purpose for which it was designed, and may at the same time be working great harm to the people who have adopted it and maintain it and trust in it—a harm which may become apparent only after a long series of years, and apparent at first, even then, only to the most careful observer. It is a familiar fact that a great change in governmental policy may not produce its full effect for many decades. We are still in the dark as to what will be the final outcome, and especially the final effect on character, of the free public educational system.

The individualist opponent of that system says that the individual is the important thing. He contends that the individual is happiest when he has the maximum of freedom; that he best develops when he most fully reaps the rewards of his own exertions and his own self-denials, and most fully receives the punishment of his own indolence and his own prodigality—of his own failure to adjust himself to men and things about him. The mass, he says, may restrain the individual who would make an attack on others; it may refuse to affiliate with the individual who does not do those things which it thinks he should do. For the mass to do more than this, he says, is so to restrict individual activity and to prevent the play of natural forces as to make impossible the development of the only kind of individuals that can form the ideal society.

This is stating it crudely. It at least suggests, however, that the advocate of liberty has on his side some of the arguments gained from the study of biology and of history. The former seems to tell us that the fittest have survived in open fight—that only by this open fight do those more fit appear; the latter seems to tell us that the better government governs the least; that the only wise thing the ruler, whether king or majority, can do for the social organism is to let it alone.

If it is of doubtful expediency, then, for the sovereign majority to take from the individual by force the means wherewith to maintain a library for the pleasure and edification of all, it is the part of wisdom to see that that library is made, as far as may be, the sure antidote to the possible bane of its origin. It must teach freedom, by its contents and by its administration. It must cultivate the individual. It must add to the joy of life. Always it must truly educate.

It is in the light of the preceding, perhaps rather doctrinaire, remarks that the following notes have been written and should be read.

The public owns its public library. This fact sheds much light on the question of public library management. It means that the public library must be fitted to public needs. It must suit its community. It must do the maximum of work at the minimum of expense. It must be an economical educational machine. It must give pleasure, for only where pleasure is is any profit taken. It must change in its manner of administration with the new time, with the new relations of books to men and of men to books. It need not altogether forget the book-worm or the belated historian, and it can take note here and there of the lover of the dodos and the freaks among printed things. But its prime purpose is to place the right books in the proper hands, to get more joyful and wise thoughts into the minds of its owners. The means of its support are taken by force from the pockets of the competent and provident; this fact should never be lost sight of. It lives in a measure by the sword. It can justify itself in this manner of securing its support only by putting into practice the familiar theory that the state, would it insure its own continuance, must see that all its citizens have access to the stores, in books, of knowledge and wisdom. It must be open to its public; it must invite its public; it must attract its public; it must please its public— all to the end that it may educate its public.

The old-time library was simply a storehouse of treasures. There were few to read books; there were few books to be read, and those few were procured at great cost of labor and time. They could be replaced when lost or stolen only with great diffi-culty, if at all, and they were guarded with exceeding care. With the cheapening of book-producing pro-cesses the reasons for this extreme safe-guarding of books disappeared. Its spirit, however, is still active. Several causes have combined to keep it alive. Even to this day there are a few books, relatively very few, which are of great value and can be replaced only with extreme difficulty or at great expense. There are also books—first editions, fine bindings, last surviving copies, and early specimens of printing —which are rightly much prized by the artist, the

17

antiquarian, the curio hunter, or the historian of handicraft. These are all most properly regarded as treasures, and are kept under lock and key. But the fact that there are a few books which should be carefully preserved from loss or injury is not sufficient cause for keeping up in these days a barrier between the public and its library. Set aside these greatly valued books and the few works highly prized for certain special reasons which the average library contains, and there is left the great body of modern books, not expensive, easily replaced, and of far more importance to ninety-nine in a hundred of any public library's constituents than all the book curios the world contains. In any save the very richest and largest libraries in this country the books which cannot be duplicated at a reasonable cost have no proper place. It is with the modern, inexpensive works that the public library chiefly concerns itself. Its art publications and its rarities of every kind can easily be disposed of in safety vaults or private rooms. Its more valuable works of reference can be guarded from any probable mutilation by a little special service. Its main collection, 60 to 80 per cent of the average library, is what the public wishes to use. These form any library's real tools in its avowed purpose of aiding in the education of the community in which it is placed.

The readers of books, moreover, are no longer few but many, and have greatly changed their manner of looking at books and the guardianship of them in the past hundred years. The tax-paying citizen to-day has his own daily or weekly paper, if nothing more, and knows well that a printed page is no longer a sacred or an expensive thing. He walks up to the shelves of the bookstore or to the counter of the news-stand and selects his own reading, under his own rules, in accordance with his own opinion of his needs, and after an actual inspection of what the shelves can afford him. He has learned, or is fast learning, that public library treasures are in the main treasures no longer; that the only rational selection of reading is one made after the examination of many books; and he is beginning to demand that he be permitted to come in immediate contact with the volumes he is invited to read. The public library, whether it be a library which the people are taxed to maintain or a library which belongs to them by gift, must, so the demand goes, be managed with as much consideration for its patrons and with as much appearance of faith in their honesty as the ready-made-clothing house or the bookstore. This demand is seconded by the new view of the functions of a public library; it is, in fact, a part of this new view. The library is no longer looked upon as a storehouse of learning, to be used by the few already learned; it is thought of as a factor in the growth of the community in wisdom, in social efficiency, and a factor therein second only to the public schools, if second even to them. It is accordingly widening its business of book distributing by the addition of the powers possible to it as a laboratory of general learning. Of books it is as true as of the materials of chemistry, botany, or biology—and even the non-literary, wayfaring man begins to see this—that only by working among them and with them can one get out of them their real worth. The public to-day, in a word, sees the importance, the absolute necessity, in fact, of the laboratory method in that study of books which underlies, or at least accompanies, the study of all other things.

In its attractiveness to the would-be student, not

to mention the desultory reader, the library whose resources are open for examination and selection is far superior to the one which keeps its patrons on the outside of the delivery desk. The book buyer finds delight in a personal inspection of the volumes he would select from. It is by the unrestrained browsing through a score of inviting volumes that the student, whether beginner or expert, finds at last the one which meets his case. To all who are drawn, whether in ignorant questioning or in enlightened zeal, to visit a collection of books, the touch of the books themselves, the joy of their immediate presence, is an inspiring thing. Those who have had experience of both methods testify that the open library gives more pleasure, encourages reading of a higher grade, and attracts more readers than the library which is closed to the public.

The cheapness of books; the growth of the public's feeling of ownership in its library, and of the propriety of laying hands on its own; a recognition of the great educational value of the laboratory method in library administration; and the widening of its field of work which a library gains by the added attraction of free access to its shelves—these considerations, save in certain peculiar cases, seem to decide the question of the proper policy of the public library toward its public. That more communities do not now demand the adoption of the system of open shelves in their public libraries is due largely to the conservatism of library boards, and to an unreasoning submission to authority on the part of the reading public. Even the enlightened are slow to ask for a right before they have exercised it and experienced its advantages.

These statements of proper library methods will

seem to the reader who is not familiar with public library methods as they are, simple, commonplace, and self-evident. He may well wonder why one takes the trouble to repeat them in print. By way of justification it should be said that the manner of conducting a public library now in almost universal use in this country is this: Between the books and the would-be users of them is placed an insurmountable physical barrier. At this barrier stand librarian and attendants. The reader or student flounders about in a list of the library's books until he arrives at a guess—it is often not more than a guess—at the titles of the books he wishes. A list of these books he hands over the barrier to the attendant, and of them the attendants brings him the first one that happens to be in. Perhaps he wishes to make a study of some subject. Generally, in such a case, he must make out a list from a brief catalogue of the books which he thinks may help him, and of the titles of articles which he surmises will be useful in files of periodicals or proceedings. This list, handed to the attendant, brings him some of the things called for. Half of them are probably not what he expected, and he must try again. Always between him and the sources of information the personality of librarian or attendant obtrudes itself. His wants must trickle over a library counter, and then must filter through the mind of a custodian who is perhaps not very intelligent and is probably not very sympathetic, before they can be satisfied by contact with the books themselves. In a good many libraries a few reference books are placed where any one can reach them. But this is in most cases the limit of the concession made to the demand for immediate contact with the library's resources. The new library in Boston has stored the most of its popular books, the books which the majority of its patrons most call for, in a dark warehouse, lighted only by artificial light, and reached, as far as the borrower is concerned, only by mechanical contrivances which compel a wait of several minutes for every book called for. The borrower cannot see the books; he cannot even see the person who does see them. He must depend on lists, telephones, pneumatic tubes, and traveling baskets—and this in the most expensive and most extensive and most famous library in the United States to-day.

What, now, the open-shelf method of administration being decided upon, should be the character of the building in which the public library is housed? The storehouse idea must be discarded at once. What is wanted is a workshop, a place for readers and students, not a safety-deposit building. The men and women who visit the library and use it—their convenience and comfort must be first consulted; how the books are to be stored is another and a secondary question. Nor can the monumental idea be for a moment maintained. The library, if it is to be a modern, effective, working institution, cannot forego the demands of its daily tenants for light, room, and air, and submit to the limitations set by calls for architectural effects, for imposing halls, charming vistas, and opportunities for decoration. The workshop, the factory, the office building, the modern business structure of almost any kind, these, rather than the palace, the temple, the cathedral, the memorial hall, or the mortuary pile, however grand, supply the examples in general accordance with which the modern book laboratory should be constructed. It is a place, is this book laboratory, in which each day hundreds and thousands of visitors must, for ten minutes or as many hours, use their eyes in reading type of all degrees of excellence and badness. First, then, every sacrifice must be made to secure all possible daylight in every corner. It is a place, again, in which many of the daily visitors will wish to go, at the same time, to the same shelves, the same cases, the same alcoves, to the same rooms, and the same desks and tables. Space—well-lighted, well-ventilated floor space—then, should be given to the public with the utmost prodigality. There is no room left, unless economy in construction and administration be entirely disregarded, for architectural display, except as it is the natural outcome of plans based primarily on utility.

The power of a library lies first in its books. Up to a certain variable limit, varying with their character and with the time and the place, quantity of books is of first importance. As the library supported by compulsory taxation is justified only as it serves to make the ignorant citizen wise and the wise citizen wiser still, its first care should be for its supply of tools—its implements for cultivating wisdom—its books. The library building, as of the second and not of the first importance, should therefore be economical in its construction. It need not be, it should not be, penurious in its appearance. To a limited extent it may speak to the passer-by of the generosity of the community, of the respect in which its builders hold the business of education. But if solid and plain and manifestly adapted to the purpose for which it is designed, it cannot well escape the attributes of dignity, and, to the reasoning observer, of beauty. The magnificent pile, to which architect and trustee can point the casual passer-by with pride, which may awe the taxpayer into forgetfulness of the contractor's bills, this has no excuse. It comes, and it promises to come often; but it is permitted by the populace in momentary forgetfulness of the public library's excuse and function, not in reasoned belief in the utility of bibliothecal palaces.

The free public library building, large or small— and of the college, university, or reference library the same may be said—so constructed as to serve thoroughly well the purposes for which it is intended, exists in theory only. It may be possible to find in this country a few small libraries in which an honest attempt has been made, with moderate success, to grapple with the library building problem. In the vast majority of cases such light as experience in library administration is able to throw on the question of the proper internal arrangement of a library building—the proper distribution of expenditure in securing room, light, ventilation, and workableness —has been simply ignored. Arguments drawn from utility, from comfort of readers and borrowers, and from economy of administration, have been set aside. Full rein often, the loose rein always, has been given to trustees' and architects' desires for architectural effect. This is the more strange because certain principles of library construction are well understood and are no longer matters for debate.

Convenient, economical, effective administration of a library calls for greater ease of access and facility of communication in the building used than does any other form of business, be it industrial, commercial, official, administrative, or religious. And this need for ease and speed in intercommunication increases rather than diminishes with the increase in the size of the library, and in the number of its patrons. Illustrations of how this general principle of library construction has been ignored may be easily found. To note the Newberry Library in Chicago and the Boston Public Library is here sufficient. Compare the accommodation possible for the busy and impatient patron—and the busy and impatient patron is one of the patrons the modern library should especially strive to serve—in these ill-adapted structures with that possible, with a few quite minor changes, in the modern tall office building, and the point is made clear at once. The whole monumental style of library architecture is almost of necessity the greatest of handicaps to library administration. It may be said, of course, that it is sometimes advisable to erect first a noble monument, then to make out of it as good a library as its monumental character permits. Granted. But it should be thoroughly understood, when such a building is up for consideration, that it is a monument, not a library. When our architects have fully seized the modern situation in its demands and its materials; when the spirit which put up the lying exteriors of the Chicago World's Fair buildings, and thereby delayed our architectural emancipation by many a long day, has begun to die out, it may be possible to erect a thoroughly useful and entirely workable building which shall be in every part a library and also an artistic monument.

The point in the free public library to which the public comes in the largest numbers is the delivery desk. The public side of this desk should be a room easy of access from the street, with cloak and toilet rooms near its entrance; well lighted, that catalogues and lists may be easily consulted, and that the work of the assistants may be done in the main without artificial light; large enough to accommodate comfortably the greatest crowd the library expects ever to attract; and so closed in that the talk and move-

LIBRARIES

ment which necessarily accompany intercourse between visitors and the library staff will not disturb
workers or readers in other parts of the library. A
corner of this room, easy of access from the desk,
should be devoted to the information desk, at which
the stranger or the student will get prompt and cour-
teous and full replies to all questions in regard to the
library's methods and resources, and suggestions in
regard to books or departments to be consulted on
any specific topic. Near this information desk
should be the desk at which borrowers' or members'
cards, permits, etc., are issued. In the delivery room,
or in a room opening from it, should be the catalogue
resources of the library. The desk should be so constructed as to serve as an aid in the transaction of
business—as a means of communication, not as a
barrier—between the assistants and the public. Near
to it and easy of access should be the books of the
lending department; nearest to it, those most used.
If for good reason it is found necessary to forbid the
public access to any part of the lending department,
it may prove advisable to place such part at some
distance from the delivery counter, and to move the
books to and fro by means of lifts, belts, or like
devices. But any plan by which the attendant, to
whom a request for certain books is made, is pre-
vented from easy access to them, stands in the way
of the library's educational work, especially where
the would-be borrower is himself denied the opportunity to see for himself, in any department, the
books he would select from. If a book asked for is
not in, another of equal or greater value on the same
subject may be in. The borrower, denied access to
the shelves, should at least have, if he wishes it, the
benefit of the attendant's knowledge of this fact. A

26

delivery service made up largely of mechanical contrivances may easily put into the hands of the public
several thousand books in a day. It may serve a
good purpose in so doing. It may find its proper
field in performing part of the book-lending work in
any large library. But it certainly cannot compete,
from an educational point of view, with a service in
which the attendant puts himself for the moment in
the inquirer's place, and himself goes to the shelves
with an intelligent interest in the inquirer's wants.

Near the desk should be the catalogue room; and
the private official catalogue of the library should be
open to the public, if possible. Such an arrangement
saves much costly duplication. It is also desirable
to have the information about the library's books
which is stored up in the catalogue room made
available for the public at short notice.

Near the delivery room and not far from the main
book room should be a special room for children, in
which may be kept all juvenile literature, so arranged
that the children may make their own choice from
the shelves. This will prove a strong attraction to
the young people, will increase their use of books of
the better class, will free other parts of the library
from the disturbance children necessarily entail, and
will save time and labor at the delivery counter.

The room for reference work, if the whole library
is not thrown open for this purpose, must be not far
from the main book room, must be near the catalogue,
and should be near the delivery counter. It should
be so planned that those who come to the library
simply for a book, or to ask a question, or on sight-
seeing, will not be compelled to pass through it.

The retiring rooms and lunch rooms for assistants,
the conversation or class rooms for special work, the

27

rooms for rough work—as mending or binding and the manual part of the preparation of books for the shelf—the periodical room, and the newspaper room can all be placed at a distance from the library's real center, the delivery counter; though the last two must be near enough to the reference room to make it easy for readers in the latter to consult the current numbers of magazines and journals.

The office of the librarian in charge should be near to the delivery room, and preferably not far from either catalogue or reference room.

The books in the public library should be selected with reference to the people who will use them. The people who make use of the free public library are, 60 per cent or more of them, readers of little but the newspapers, the popular magazine, and novels. The reading room should supply, and generously, the newspaper and the periodical. The circulating department should put much thought and much energy into fiction. The fiction shelves, perhaps above all others, should be open to the public. If they are thus open, the question of how low in the scale of literature the library must descend in its selection of novels to attract as many readers as its income will permit it to supply will almost solve itself. Liberty to go to a collection of novels, embracing the best works of the best writers of all countries and all ages, will be attraction enough. It will not be necessary to put on the shelves books of the Southworth, the Roe, and the Mary J. Holmes school to draw to the library the ignorant and inexperienced. Such readers are wedded to their literary idols, not because they find them best, but because they know no others. They will not often take the evidence of expert or of catalogue

2S

that there are other good novels than those of which they have heard from fellow-readers. But the book itself of the unknown writer, placed in easy reach, with attractive title, cover, and illustrations, will prove irresistible. Liberty to see, touch, peep into, and taste the new and heretofore untried will set the known and the unknown on the same plane in the mind of the inexperienced; and the unknown, if the better book and if selected with an eye to the library's constituency, will gain the day. The horizon of the inexperienced reader will, in such a library, soon widen. The devotee of mush and slush will, under her own guidance, following her own sweet will, almost unconsciously rise to a higher plane. She will be proud to think that she has found possibilities of pleasure in good authors whom she herself has had the wit to discover. The fiction list then will not be long and will be select. Two thousand titles, many times duplicated, will cover the field.

With the shelves open, with full liberty of choice given, the obliging attendant will be all the more appreciated. He will obtrude no opinions and no advice, but will be ready and able to give both, if asked, or if opportunity offers. He will be supplemented with catalogues. And just as the library will make its fiction department—the department in which it will first reach, by which perhaps it can alone reach, from 60 to 80 per cent of its visitors—the most attractive and most carefully administered of all, so will it for this department best equip itself with aids and guides. It will have here catalogues of the most varied kinds—special lists, descriptive lists, like those of Griswold; historical lists, like that of the Boston Public Library; annotated lists, like that of the San Francisco Public Library; critical journals; and books and essays on the novel, its development and uses. In addition to all these things, it will tell the inquirer in which novels he can find set forth great historical characters and the prominent personages of fiction; in which he will find descriptions of notable scenes and historical events; in which are found rare psychological analyses, striking descriptions that have become part of the everyday life of the cultivated; and discussions of social, political, and religious questions; and which novels will best tell him of life in this city, in that country, on the sea. In a word, the public's free public library will recognize at last the public's demand for the novel; will not attempt to excuse it, to hide it, to make light of it, or to counteract it; but will make use of it as an educational force in itself, and as a point of departure to more serious things. The novel reader is not a hopeless case. If he be a confirmed novel reader and nothing more, he has at least the reading habit, and in his youth can in most cases be led from that habit to question and to think.

The reference room of the free public library is in some sort already here. Not a few libraries recognize the reasonableness of a demand on the public's part for access to dictionaries, encyclopedias, atlases, gazetteers, and the like. Under the modern view the whole library becomes, of course, a great reference room. But the reference department proper, even in the modern public library, should contain ample accommodations in the way of desks, tables, writing materials, etc., for the casual inquirer or the student.

In other departments the wants of the reader, the

beginner in learning, should be first supplied, books for the specialist being added as rapidly and to as great an extent as actual demand makes advisable and funds in hand make possible. No money should be expended on mere literary curios or on historical knickknacks. The historical society and the antiquary can look after these things, and should not have the public purse for their competitor.

In accordance with the general spirit of the open-shelf method of administration, great liberality should be shown in the issuing of library cards. To the library itself for purposes of reference every one who applies will, of course, be admitted, so he be clean and reputable in appearance. To become an accredited borrower of books from the library one should be asked to do no more than sign some simple form of agreement. This, in addition to the information which can be obtained from a few questions put by librarian or assistants, with perhaps a reference to the city directory, has proved to be enough in actual practice to prevent the issuing of cards to people who wish them simply to make way with the library's books. In spite of this fact, the custom still holds in most libraries of demanding not only the signature of the person who wishes to become a borrower to an elaborate contract—this signature to be written at the library itself—but also the signature of some accredited citizen who agrees to become responsible for the borrower himself. This is entirely unnecessary. The additional clerical work involved in the keeping of the two sets of names of borrowers and guarantors of borrowers, together with the labor necessitated by looking them up in directories and elsewhere, will cost more, save in

31

very exceptional cases, than will the books which may be lost through the adoption of extreme liberality in the issuing of borrowers' cards. The people's money in this part of its library's administration, as in every other, should be spent rather in extending and making more easily accessible to the average citizen the library's resources than in setting barriers of red tape between the books and the people who own them and wish to use them.

THE FAILURE OF BOOK REVIEWING

Springfield, Mass., Republican, May 23, 1900

It is part of a librarian's business to know something about new books, to know enough about them to enable him to decide wisely which of them to buy for a public library. Of course, in very many cases some one whose judgment he can rely on, better posted in a special line than any librarian can possibly be in all lines, decides for him. This is especially true of technical works. But there are still left many books on which he must form an opinion from reviews in the literary journals. And so the librarian reads a good many reviews. Most librarians probably do not get much beyond the reviews, with perhaps a look at the title pages of the books in question, if he sees them at all, and sometimes with a luxurious dip into the table of contents. In reading reviews—I am speaking now of reviews of "literary" books, not of scientific or technical works—many librarians are impressed, I am sure, with the small amount of really helpful knowledge to be got from most of them. By helpful knowledge I mean here such information about a book as the librarian needs to make a wise decision on the question of its purchase. From the formal entry in the trade journal he can learn, of course, of the title, the author, the publisher, the price, the size in inches, the number of pages, if bound or not, and perhaps the number of maps and illustrations. But this is only the skeleton. Rather it is simply the skin of the book, which the publisher offers duly stretched into the semblance of a thing of value. It may be stuffed with straw, or padded out with sawdust, or possibly it covers the

33

living bone, sinew and muscle of a book that is a book. To find out what may be within the fair exteriors of the latest thing out—this is where the difficulty lies. And here is where the literary journals affect to serve us—and commonly do not. They do not even set forth all the facts as to the book's physique, its bodily condition. They uniformly withhold information as to the paper on which it is printed, whether it is cheap wood pulp which will not stand three weeks' honest wear, or heavily coated with clay, and therefore helpless against even the quiet turning of its leaves, or made on honor and planned for a decent lifetime of usefulness. They do not tell us if it is bound in a thorough, workmanlike way, or is thrown together with just enough of muslin and glue to keep it in shape until it is sold. The type, the ink, the index, the margins, the page illustrations—generally ready to fall out before the book has been once read—these things they say nothing about. And to the library they are very important, and especially so to the expense side of its accounts in new copies, repairs and binding.

All these matters, to be sure, the librarian can judge of himself, with some slight degree of accuracy, if he can handle the book before he buys it, which often he cannot. But to be able to learn them from the reviews, where common sense would say they should be set forth, would be a very helpful thing.

The book's physique, however, is, after all, not as important as its character. And in telling us of this the literary journals fail to live up to that which they profess. Every new book they mention is excellent. If one reads with credulous mind the things said by most reviewers about most books one would feel that an Augustan age of letters comes round again with every rising sun. To test this statement a little I have gone over all the longer notices of books in four literary journals for two months. The journals examined were the Bookbuyer, the Bookman, the Critic and the Nation. The first two are publishers' organs, and perhaps it would be asking too much that they should do anything but praise their own books and for the sake of peace refrain from condemnation of those of rival publishers. But if this is their policy they should not cultivate quite so sedulously the air of fairness and breadth. And of the purely literary journals like the Critic, which must support itself largely by the advertising in one column of the books it professes to criticise with unbiased mind in the next, it is perhaps seeking grapes of thorns to expect unterrified censure. But the three are in large measure typical, in this country at least, of the journals to which the book-buyer must turn for information on the latest books. The Nation, as the returns of my brief examination indicate, is almost in another class, and helps to relieve American book reviewing of the full measure of condemnation.

In the four journals considered there were, in the two months' issues which were examined, 243 reviews. In the Critic 75, with about 470 words in each; in the Bookman 54, with 570 words in each; in the Bookbuyer 60, with 500 words in each; and in the Nation 54, with 1,020 words in each. These 54 reviews in the Nation do not include a large number of shorter notes, such as would be ranked as reviews proper in the other three journals, each containing 100 to 300 words. The greater length of the Nation's reviews is not due to simple prolixity. They are in general stronger as well as longer than the others. Of these reviews those dealing with fiction were in the Critic 28 per cent, in the Bookman

50 per cent, in the Bookbuyer 37 per cent, and in the Nation none.

Had my examination happened to cover one of the months in which the Nation's novel reader does up with a vigorous hand a batch of recent fiction, these figures would have been different. But it would still have been true that in that journal an unusually small amount of space is given to novels. Dividing these 243 criticisms of recent books into four classes, those which very warmly praise; those which moderately praise, but very lightly, if at all, condemn; those which take the aggravating middle ground, blowing neither hot nor cold, simply prattling; and those which frankly condemn, we get these results:

Journal	Total reviews	High praise	Some praise	Saying nothing	Condemn
Critic	75	40	15	17	3
Bookbuyer	60	31	20	4	5
Bookman	54	39	9	5	1
Nation	54	31	8	1	14

All, it will be seen, with the exception of the Nation, lack the courage of condemnation. And of the 189 works examined by the three first named, 154 are found excellent and only nine are actually disapproved of.

This table tells the story of American literary criticism. It is a chorus of praise. Of course it may be said that literary journals do not deign to notice books that they feel they cannot rightly praise. But they review the popular literature of the day, the books that are talked about, offered for sale everywhere and read by intelligent people; and to suppose that all these are worthy of a tithe of the praise they get from professional reviewers is simply absurd.

FAILURE OF BOOK REVIEWING

Book reviews are written to please authors—and publishers. It is a pity, but it's true. Occasionally a journal fails to catch the drift of things and condemns the wrong book. The Bookman's one condemnation in its ocean of praise was directed against "David Harum." Later the editor wrote a very flattering estimate of the book in another journal, when the tide had turned strongly in its favor.

A good book review—I am not speaking here of "criticism" in the broader sense of the word—should tell the busy book buyer and the busy reader who wants to know about the books he cannot read or even see, these things:

What the book is about; with what authority the author speaks; what part of his field he covers; with what degree of definiteness he covers it; the relation his work bears to others in the same or cognate fields; if it is well arranged; if it is a book for the student and specialist or for the general reader.

By a man who knows his subject, these things can be told in a few words. They are told in the columns of the Nation and a few other journals not infrequently. Generally the reviewers do not set them forth, and sad experience leads the reader to feel that the study of book reviews simply leads him astray. They generally darken counsel.

An illustration of how books ought to be reviewed —ought to be, that is, if the reviews are to be helpful guides in book-buying—is found in the admirable "List of books for girls and women and their clubs," compiled by George Iles. The work was largely done by experts. They felt they were untrammeled by an advertising agent, and they spoke their minds. It is a pity there is not more such work available.

A LIBRARIAN'S ENTHUSIASM

Bulletin of the New Hampshire Library Commission,
March, 1901

I have known many librarians and library assistants, old and young, and every one of them has testified, directly or indirectly, to keen delight in his work. Few leave the profession and they always with regrets. The work is not easy and the pay is not large.

Our calling would seem to have strong attractions for people of a certain type—and so it has. Of the many which may be mentioned I wish to speak here of two only: the opportunities it offers for the promotion of happiness, and its wide variety of interests. Attractive careers in the field of altruism are not open to every one. The world's work must be done. That it may be done well, those most competent must do it. That the most competent may do it, they must compete with the less competent, and must win the day. Here, then, are war, victory, defeat, and the spoils of conquest. Nature, red in tooth and claw, comes perforce into every factory and every market, and comes to stay. Sympathy softens the aspect of this strife and tempers the sufferings of the defeated. But the strife goes on; and neither legislative enactment nor public opinion, even though born of generous sentiments, can stop it; and if they are carried beyond a certain point, they but forbid the supremacy of the most competent and work us harm. Business must be done; most must engage in business; therefore, most must do battle day by day.

But, if libraries are good things, and it is impossible now to question this; and if free, tax-supported libraries are good things, and to-day it is not easy to question this; then we have in the librarian's calling a field in which competition is simply a joyful one over efficiency in good works. It is not—and this cannot be said too often—a question of making others good. They who are much given to improving the low morals of others are already Pharisees. The whole question of librarianship is one of joy, of pleasure, of fullness of life, of happiness. If the librarian of the country village, for example, can see that her little collection of books, under her clever rule, subtly fitted to its owners, wisely meeting the needs its own active presence arouses, makes this one and that one, old and young, here and there, see more things, know of more things, care for more things, take the broader view, loose the bond of bigotry, open the eyes of charity, teach "of course" to wait upon "perhaps," change self-satisfaction to ambition, and add sparkle to the daily grind—then, is she not a friend of society and of some good in the world?

This mere mention of the character of the librarian's career, shows it at once to be helpfully unselfish in its essence, as few careers in the world's field of work can be. It calls attention, also, to the second of the two attractive features in the librarian's calling which I wish here to emphasize: the variety of its interests. All knowledge is the librarian's province. None can explore this domain thoroughly, but any one can realize, if only vaguely, its immensity, can look upon it reverently and can venture, with timorous delight, into a corner here and there. Some one should write us an essay, or perhaps a poem, on "Our Pleasure in the Books We Cannot Read!" What joy there is, as we walk among the shelves, in the contemplation of the knowledge and wisdom that

we know lie here, and there! Some day we shall
have the "Ballad of Him who Joyed to Know that
Others Knew."

And the work to be done! First, in the library
itself; no matter how small it may be, the librarian
gets pleasure in applying to its management every
latest method of arrangement, classification, cataloguing, shelving, delivery, access, that she finds by
careful study applies to her peculiar case. It soon
takes on for her the air of a home. She says of it:
That which my people enjoy when they visit my home
fireside, that they shall find and enjoy here. Light,
fresh air, adornment, neatness, refinement, hospitality, cheer—in all these things my library shall rival
the most attractive home in the town which owns it.
This is not an office, or a store, or a factory; it is
the chosen home of the good and wise men who wrote
these books; it is constituted and maintained to help
my fellow villagers to find life easier and brighter
and more worth the living; it shall speak at once to
every comer of all these things. This is home-making
and library management—two of the best and most
delightful of occupations, both in one.

Looking abroad, she sees the editor, the preacher,
the teacher, and the scholar, and says at once: These
are all on my side and must work with me. Their
work is not mine, but mine is surely a part of theirs.
She finds they meet her halfway, and more. Her
books have allies in their work. They become mobile
and move through the community on the wings of a
few words spoken shrewdly here and there by these
their friends.

The pulpit speaks and the press and the teacher,
and clubs and Sunday schools and sociables; and
every chance gathering of friends takes up the words,

and the treasures on her shelves come forth and move about among the people, and their mission is accomplished, and the library has wellwishers, and advocates and promoters and benefactors.

And the children come, to the very youngest; for no one has discovered that good books hurt children, and children who hurt books are few and easily cured.

Thus, with all knowledge for her province, with old and young of every kind and of every trade and calling in her community for her field of work, and the promotion of human happiness for her aim, the librarian takes up her daily task each morning with enthusiasm and lays it down each night with regret.

WHAT WE READ

Printed, in Part, in World's Work, March, 1902

What is it that the people read? First, of course, the newspapers. There are published in a twelve-month in this country about 4,500 different books. The total number of volumes issued in a year is perhaps 10,000,000. Add to these the several million volumes, the output of previous years, found in libraries, and we have a brave show of possibility of book reading. But it is very largely a possibility. A few hundred thousand people read novels, a less number read other books. A few use books in their profession, more simply think they are going to read books and rarely do. Books in these days are for pleasure, for profit and for pride of possession. But newspapers are read. Newspapers have readers—or die. They often create a demand, but unless the readers continue the demand the supply must cease. No newspaper is read from end to end by any one of its readers. But all of every issue of every newspaper, take them by and large, is read by many people. Again demand and supply give us our proof. The paper prints two kinds of things, two kinds from its own point of view—the news and views the people wish to read, and the announcements which advertisers wish to have printed. The first kind of print is read, or it would not appear; the second kind is read or the advertiser would find his money wasted and would advertise no more. All of all newspapers, this is the people's reading. And in considering the gross amount of reading of newspapers going on among us to-day it is not enough to count simply the number of copies of all papers published; the number of persons who read each copy must be taken into consideration. Nothing but a guess is possible. Mine is one and a half readers for every copy. This seems modest. It would be difficult to prove that it is an overestimate.

From the total population deduct children under fourteen, illiterates and a few other small non-reading classes, and there remain about 40,000,000 adults who could read periodicals if they would. About four billion separate copies of periodicals of all kinds are printed in this country every year, one hundred to each possible reader. But many, probably a large majority of the people who work in mills, mines, factories and on farms read very little, though a goodly proportion read something. On the other hand, the professional and managing classes read many more than a hundred a year. Any reader of this who runs over a brief list of his more intimate friends, will find each reads, if only hastily, between three hundred and a thousand. Instead, then, of having forty million people reading one hundred periodicals in a year, we have probably not more than half that number reading on an average twice as many.

From the directories of newspapers and other periodicals of the United States, I have compiled the statistics given in the following tables that show how many dailies, weeklies and monthlies are published in this country today. They show also how many copies are issued in a year of the periodicals in each of these classes.

From among the many newspapers in the country, I selected a few as fairly typical, and took one copy of each of these few, published on days when no unusual space was given to any especially promi-

nent topic. The contents of these typical newspapers I analyzed, and having made allowance for
room taken by illustrations, by display advertisements, and by display headings on news articles,
tabulated their contents in accordance with the sched-
ule given below. The analysis is only tentative of
course. An analysis of another group of papers
published on different dates would show results different from these. But the difference in results
would come rather in minor details than in the general outline.

We may quite safely assume that four billion and
a half copies of daily and weekly papers published
within twelve months in this country are devoted to
the topics listed in the table on page 46, somewhat in
the proportion indicated. Reducing the contents of
these newspapers, or the words in them, to volumes
of the size of "David Harum," we have in another
column a statement of the number of volumes of
"David Harum" size that appear in newspaper form
each year in this country, on the several subjects
indicated in the table.

The number of daily, weekly and monthly copies
of periodicals published in the United States every
year is: dailies, 2,865,466,000; weeklies, 1,208,190,000;
monthlies, 263,452,000; total, 4,337,108,000 copies.

My figures are taken from a reliable newspaper
directory. Other estimates, based on returns direct
from the publishers themselves, are nearly twice as
large as mine.

In another table I have restated the situation,
grouping some of the thirty-two topics of the first
table, reducing thereby the number of classes to five.
Again putting the contents of the newspapers of a
year into volumes of "David Harum" size we have

LIBRARIES

SPACE DEVOTED TO VARIOUS SUBJECTS

		Per Cent of Space (Approx.)	Space in Terms of a Book the Size of "David Harum" Copies
1.	Commercial and financial: including market and manufacturing reports, real estate, etc.	14	270,600,000
2.	Health and pleasure resorts; general gossip; trivial town news	8	160,200,000
3.	Advertisements: dry goods, clothing, department stores, etc.	8	159,200,000
4.	Political: domestic, army and navy, Congress, Philippine War, etc.	8	156,600,000
5.	Sports: athletics, etc.	7	132,000,000
6.	Legal: trials, colonial questions, notices, etc.	6	119,000,000
7.	Criminal	4	86,200,000
8.	Personal: not trivial	3½	71,400,000
9.	Advertisements: personal, marriages, deaths, employment wanted	3½	69,600,000
10.	Advertisements: medical	3	61,200,000
11.	Advertisements: railroads, shipping, telephone, telegraph, hotels, etc.	3	60,000,000
12.	Advertisements: wants	3	58,000,000
13.	Advertisements: real estate, lodgings, resorts	3	56,400,000
14.	Literature: essays, stories, poetry, book reviews, drawing, music and art	2½	51,000,000
15.	Social science: strikes, unions, reform work, etc.	2½	49,400,000
16.	Advertisements: financial, stocks, etc.	2½	49,400,000
17.	Religion: churches and church work	2⅓	47,600,000
18.	Political: foreign, including wars	2½	46,400,000
19.	Railroads; shipping news; trolley lines, etc.	2¼	45,000,000
20.	Disasters	2	41,000,000
21.	"Society"	2	41,000,000
22.	Science	2	40,000,000
23.	Political: international, Chinese crisis, Nicaragua Canal, etc.	1½	30,200,000
24.	Advertisements: theatre, opera and other entertainments	1	21,200,000
25.	Educational: schools, colleges	1	18,800,000
26.	Advertisements: food and mineral waters...	¾	15,000,000
27.	Theatrical: actual stage news	½	13,400,000
28.	Musical	½	12,600,000
29.	Advertisements: books	½	9,000,000
30.	Advertisements: fine arts, schools, etc.	¼	3,900,000
31.	Historical	⅙	3,600,000
32.	Advertisements: liquors	⅛	3,200,000

Note—Twenty-eight per cent or 566,000,000 volumes is advertising.

another estimate of the number of volumes of each of these broader classes that are read by the people of the United States every twelve months.

SUMMARY OF OUTPUT OF PERIODICALS

		Copies of "David Harum"
1.	Political and governmental matters	352,200,000
2.	Criminal sensational and trivial....	287,400,000
3.	Intellectual, scientific and religious	248,200,000
4.	Personal and social................	572,800,000
5.	Business	539,400,000
	Total...........................	2,000,000,000

The weekly papers I have not included in this general analysis. They produce in a year 1,208,190,000 copies, a little more than one-third of the output of the dailies, and probably somewhat smaller in size on the average. An analysis of them would be still more difficult than has been the analysis of the dailies, for the reason that among the weeklies are to be found a large number of periodicals which are not newspapers proper, ranging in quality from journals like the Police Gazette, the Nickel libraries and cheap story papers to the Youth's Companion, the Outlook, and countless trade and technical journals. The quality of the literature published in the weeklies is probably on the whole not much if at all superior to that found in the dailies. Weekly publications of what we commonly call the better class, would bring up the average, while sporting journals and cheap story papers and things of that kind would tend to bring it down again to the level of the field covered by daily publications.

Monthlies number a total output in a year of 285,000,000, only 6 per cent of the grand total. Some of them are very widely read. The number of readers of each monthly is probably greater than the number of readers of the weeklies and dailies, but in spite of this fact, when one considers the things read by the people of this country, monthly and quarterly journals may be almost left out of account.

The scope of the influence of various kinds of periodical publications is shown in the following table, which shows the extent to which the various kinds of journals are read. The papers are classified according to circulation:

Daily Circulation	Dailies	Weeklies	Monthlies
Over 75,000	1,635,425,000	85,800,000	172,800,000
Over 40,000	350,560,000	70,720,000	22,080,900
Over 20,000	350,560,000	111,280,000	22,080,000
Over 17,500	109,550,000	38,220,000	8,220,000
Over 12,500	156,400,000	53,300,000	10,500,000
Over 7,500	14,085,000	68,250,000	12,150,000
Over 4,000	179,036,000	76,900,000	10,800,000
Over 2,000	40,690,000	312,600,000	4,800,000
All under 2,000 rated at 600	29,160,000	391,120,000	22,000
	2,865,466,000	1,208,190,000	263,452,000

From these figures it is difficult to make generalizations or draw conclusions. This is the newspaper age. The mere physical and psychical effects of reading, increased as it has been so tremendously in the last quarter of a century, is probably materially affecting us. Just how, nobody seems to know. This is something for the physiologists and psychologists to tell us about. The effect on the minds of the people of this country and Europe of assimilating this enormous amount of reading matter each year must certainly be great. A hundred years from now the historian may be able to point to the last quarter of the nineteenth century as the period during which were brought forth, through the medium of the daily papers, the causes which profoundly affected the history of the twentieth century.

WHAT WE READ

Is it possible to learn by experience and observation how to overcome the monster of print? Some learn this. Those who survive in the struggle to-day must learn how not to be dominated by printed things. Perhaps only by experience in life can it be learned at all, but education, which claims to be a preparation for life itself, could devote itself in large measure to fitting those who receive it to struggle successfully with the monster of the printing press.

To put it more exactly, the children in the schools —could they not have simple, practical illustrations, largely of course experiential, in the use of the newspaper and other periodicals? They are taught to read, and they are taught much beyond this. In the best schools they are taught a good deal beyond this. They are given instruction about authors and books of past times, authors and books of whom the majority will never hear again. Should they not be given a few hints at least as to the way in which they can best make use of the printed things they will actually come in contact with, first the daily paper, next a weekly with cheap pictures, next a serial publication devoted to silly stories? If education is preparation for life would it not be advisable to give to young people a little specific preparation for the large portion of their lives which will be spent in contact with the daily printed page?

LIBRARY PROBLEMS

Pedagogical Seminary, June, 1902

Gabriel Naudé had charge of the library of Cardinal Mazarin and of the libraries of other notable people in the seventeenth century. When he was about twenty-five years of age, in 1627, he published a little volume which he called "Advice on the management of a library." This was at the beginning of his career as a book lover and librarian. Yet even at that age and before he had yet enjoyed the experience of gathering and arranging some of the most notable libraries in the Europe of that day, he approached his subject with a fullness of mind and breadth of view which are not often found among librarians. In the closing chapter of his little book he speaks of the proper purpose of a library. The acquisition, classification and general care of it he has duly described in previous chapters. "All these matters," he says, "having been settled, there remains to the completion of this discussion only a statement of what should be the library's chief end and aim. To suppose that after all the care and expense I have heretofore suggested have been given to the accumulation of many books and their proper installation, we may, as it were, hide all their lights beneath a bushel, may condemn all the brave spirits they embody to eternal silence and solitude—this is to fail utterly to understand the purpose of a library. Of a library we may say, as Seneca says of Nature, that she 'desires not merely to be looked at, but also to be admired; that she would lose all the fruits of her labor, were she to exhibit her handiwork, so vast, so noble, so subtly complex, so bright, and so beautiful in ways so manifold, to solitude alone.' In vain would one follow the instructions I have set forth and incur the large expense I have recommended in the purchase of books and their proper establishing, if he have not in mind their consecration to public use; if it is in his heart ever to refuse access to them to the humblest who may have need of them."

These sentiments were uttered 275 years ago. They have not obtained very wide acceptance yet; because the preservative function of a library, for several hundred years so justly prominent, has persisted like an old, fixed habit, and made difficult the development of other functions which changed conditions demand.

All people are becoming readers. The newspaper, in the past three decades, has raised the number of those in this country who make use of print for recreation and information, from two or three million to perhaps ten million. There are among us at least thirty million more persons preparing to come into the ranks of readers. And every day the newspaper gathers more and prints more of all that touches life, and sells that more for less and less, and encroaches on the domain which the book and the weekly, monthly, and quarterly magazine once held for their own. Books cost less and less each year to make; writers increase in number both relatively and absolutely; and books of all kinds, from simple restatements of trivial facts to careful announcements of the results of prolonged research, from silly verse to masterpieces of imaginative writing, rush through the press in an endless and swelling flood. Formerly, save for oral tradition, only in rare and costly books were to be found the means of culture, and the secrets of the arts, trades and professions. Now the classics and the literature of information are to be had almost for the asking. Libraries designed to serve the needs of many decades to come prove too small before they are fairly occupied. Books overflow the shelves; readers crowd the floors.

In the great city, as well as in the small towns, donors, trustees, librarians and architects seem not to face these facts of modern life in the field of paper, print and readers. They build after old precedents. They accumulate books as did our fathers when the material, the paper, print and binding, of the book itself was rare and costly. They provide for the few who read forty years ago instead of for the multitudes who read today, and they administer as if library science were an art preservative instead of an art descriptive, selective, directive and distributive.

Much has been done, to be sure, to meet the new demands this increase of books and papers make upon us. Library methods have changed. We need go back only twenty-five years to find the original, natural and in its early days entirely just view of a library's proper character and method in general acceptance. The librarian's art was then an art preservative. Books were to be kept, kept jealously, and used carefully, and only by a selected few. Library buildings were storehouses. The space in them for books was relatively generous, that for readers or users of books relatively small. Lofty rooms with encircling galleries satisfied the demand for show. The questions of heating, lighting, ventilation and shelving were secondary and unconsidered, or not well considered. The coming tide of books and the coming hordes of readers were unforeseen, and all buildings were designed to invite and encourage a growth they could not satisfy. Many a city, town and college in those days built for a decade or two only, when they believed they were building for generations. Things are better today. But few yet realize the full extent of the changes time has wrought in the world of books, and very few library buildings have been erected in full realization of what the changed conditions demand.

It is impossible to draw up general rules as to the details of library construction. The factors of funds, location, adjoining buildings and special needs, all must be given weight in each individual case. A few general principles are, however, of almost universal application.

Libraries always grow faster than their communities suppose they will. Probably nine out of ten of all the library buildings put up in this country have already proved to be too small. Books will increase in number more rapidly each succeeding year. Popular education and cheap newspapers are rapidly increasing the number of readers and of library users in every community. The first general rule, then is, make the building as large as the funds permit. Defer decoration if need be; but get abundant floor space by all means, and provide for extensions if possible.

The public buildings in this country over twenty-five years old which are still fit—in location, style, construction and arrangement—for the purposes for which they were intended are very few. Do not, then, look forward to great permanence for your library building, and do not think it necessary to make it absolutely fire-proof at the cost of size and convenience. Books can be reasonably well insured. Save in a few large collections a total loss is not a vital thing. Build substantially; but do not imagine your structure is for all time, or even for a hundred years, when twenty-five will probably find it out of date, out of place, and a burden.

A library is a place in which many people are to read every day. Give them all the light you can.

Library methods have entirely changed in the past ten years. We may be sure they will further change in the next twenty-five. What the changes will be, no one knows. The buildings adapted to the methods of ten years ago are to-day out of date. They are hindrances to development and to good work. We may be sure that buildings especially adapted to the methods of to-day will prove to be poorly adapted to the methods of 1925, and the closer we fit them to present needs by permanent construction the more out of date they will prove to be as new needs arise. Therefore, make your building adaptable to new conditions. Provide all the well-lighted floor space you can, and let it alone. Avoid permanent partitions. Do not be deluded into surrounding each spot on which a certain kind of work or reading is to be carried on, with a wall of brick or stone. Why should one who reads the Nineteenth Century be separated by a huge light and air excluding, distance-increasing partition from one who consults an encyclopedia, or examines a catalogue, or studies engravings? The need of partitions to keep out noise from other parts of the library is much less than most suppose. Time will try all division walls inside your library, and prove most of them wrong. Leave them out, and get better air and light; greater ease of administration at less cost; greater comfort for the public; more available floor space—two rooms each twenty feet square are not nearly as large in actual utility as is one room 20x40 feet—and an elasticity, a responsiveness to future needs, which the next generation will thank you for.

With this no-partition rule goes the rule against fixtures. Complete your interior. Then add the fittings and cases as they are needed and move them, when occasion arises, as time goes on. Fixed desks, fixed rails, fixed bookcases, save perhaps in a stack, are obstacles to comfortable administration. No delivery desk was ever built right the first time. Therefore, build it so it can easily be changed. The books outside the stack will increase in number; so will your readers. This increase will compel the shifting of cases for the former and of tables for the latter. Make all furniture in small pieces and all movable.

Put as much as possible of the floor space on one level. Stairs are bad in any library. The smaller the library the worse they are. They mean additional attendants; they add to the daily labor; they are not grateful to the public.

The essential things, then, in library construction are maximum of space, on the fewest possible floors, good light, a minimum of partitions, and no fixtures. Many libraries have been built in recent years; probably not a dozen among them conform to these conditions. This is, in part, the fault of librarians, who have not realized the future of their own calling; in part, of trustees, who have valued things they thought magnificent, "tasty," "elegant," and imposing before the needs of their constituency; in part, of architects who let convention and precedent rule in interior arrangement as well as in exterior design. The sins of the father are visited on the children in such buildings as those of the Boston public and the Columbia college libraries, which by their very cost and prominence strengthen the evil determinations of many an architect and board.

LIBRARY PROBLEMS

The old librarian was often master of his books. He knew them, every one. Each stood for years in its accustomed place and was in the librarian's mind like an ancient landmark. But the incoming tide increased: the old librarian passed and his knowledge went with him. Careful lists were needed. As lists grew they became complex. Rules of cataloguing arose and flourished. The need for grouping on the shelves books of like nature was soon apparent. Classification became a necessity. Its complexity increased. And the classing of books and the listing of books, and the listing of parts of books and the printing of these lists, which were in fact indexes to whole libraries of books—seemed imperative, and libraries exhausted their resources in printing catalogues which were out of date before their proofs were read, and projected card catalogues which time may prove to be bibliothecal Frankensteins.

Yet the development of this inventory-and-index idea in library management was natural and proper. It has been of great assistance in bringing libraries under control. We look forward, however, and see that we are not yet at the end of the matter. New difficulties born of the very profusion of books, promise to arise. Its many books and its expanding catalogues threaten to obscure our vision of the library itself. In twenty years, libraries of one or two million volumes will be considered as only in their infancy. Within the lifetime of some of the younger members of the profession, libraries of a few hundred thousand volumes will be as common as were those of a few tens of thousands a quarter of a century ago. The library of a million volumes will need for its indexing, under present methods, five million cards.

Without going into details, we can see how cumbrous will be a catalogue of this size, no matter how carefully it is arranged. Its form is abhorrent to many practical men who make use of books. The ignorant cannot use it, the learned do not need it. It is a tedious and irritating task to finger cards. In a large catalogue the entry of the latest book, and the vast majority of those who use books want first of all the last book issued on their subject, is lost in a vast desert of useless references. Men of moderate intelligence, occasional visitors to the library, are helpless in the presence of the catalogue and turn in despair to the attendant, who often depends himself more on lists and special bibliographies than on the catalogue. The student, versed in books, hunts out his own authorities and asks of the catalogue little more than the information that the library has or has not certain volumes. He perhaps can go to it for a few of the first steps of the investigation he is about to set out upon; but having taken those first few steps, he wishes to go direct to the books themselves. In fact, few men who wish to consult books on a certain topic care for more than guidance to the books. No card catalogue can give them the information they need. They wish the books themselves; the footnotes and indexes in the books themselves. They go from point to point in their own way, each consulting his own particular needs. The catalogue for them is hardly more than a starting point. It is not much more than a means of laying hands on a certain book when once they have learned that that certain book is the one they wish to see. The specialist finds more helpful than the catalogue a few minutes conversation with some one connected with the library and posted on the literature of the subject he is about to investigate. Such a person in a general way outlines the range of the library's resources, and puts him in touch with the subject if he is not so already, and indicates the location of the books he may wish to consult. Each year, as the output of books grows larger and as they become cheaper, the number each library can and must buy will increase and the annual additions to the cards in the catalogue will become greater in number. This will add to the expense. If the Library of Congress succeeds in its admirable plan of printing correct cards, purchasable at a small price by all libraries, this will reduce the original cost of the catalogue; but it will induce many libraries to add rapidly to their number of cards and so will add to the cost of their storage and arrangement. The labor of sorting a thousand new cards into their proper places among a million others is immense. This labor increases for every library each year and will become for many small libraries a burden larger than they now anticipate.

Nor is this all. Not only is the catalogue becoming an alarmingly expensive creation; not only is it growing more cumbersome to the user; not only does it contain each year a greater and greater amount of chaff—its cards referring to the dead books—relatively to the few grains of wheat—its cards referring to the live books; but also it becomes as it grows an institution more and more difficult to revise. In most cases it must in time be revised. Librarians in hundreds of towns and smaller cities—and I believe in most large cities also—will soon find their shelf-space full. They will keep on buying books, more in number each year. They must make room for them. They will pronounce judgment on many of the older volumes and say that for their library

those books are dead. They will give them away, sell
them or burn them. But the dead books are entered
in the catalogue, on the shelf-list and in the accession
books. And the labor of removing from the catalogue and its allied lists all traces of the books pronounced dead and sent away is prodigious. Yet it
must be carried through. I am not attempting to
solve the problem I am presenting. I venture only
to sound a warning.

President Eliot, of Harvard, says it is time for
libraries to begin to discriminate between the living
and the dead among books. He asks for new methods
of treatment. It is well that one who speaks with
authority says what many have been saying for
several years. It is not too soon to attack this
problem.

Add to President Eliot's appeal for a change from
the hoarding process to the method of elimination
the bold statement by President Harper of Chicago
University as to the place the library is to occupy
in the educational institutions of the future—and his
prophecies apply with equal force to the public
library and its special community—and you have
ample justification for the distinction already made
in this paper between the former function of
libraries—the preservation of books—and its latter
day functions, of evaluation, selection, direction and
distribution.

President Harper says: "The library and the
laboratory have already practically revolutionized
the methods of higher education. In the really modern institution, the chief building is the library. . . .
The librarian is one of the most learned members of
the faculty; in many instances, certainly the most
influential. . . . The library, fifty years ago almost

unknown, today already the center of the institution's intellectual activity, half a century hence with its sister, the laboratory, almost equally unknown fifty years ago, will have absorbed all else, and will have become the institution itself." Public as well as university libraries, as they develop into the influential institutions which President Harper says they are to become, will change much from what they now are. Just what are the changes they will undergo, it is impossible to prophesy. They have been indicated, we may reasonably suppose, by the changes they have undergone in the past few years. Their buildings, as already suggested, will become simpler, better adapted to economical administration, more easily modified to suit new needs, and more readily enlarged for increasing use.

Cataloguing methods will be simplified and cheapened. Some way must be discovered of making at least an author index which can be more easily kept up to date, more easily and more quickly used, and more readily changed by the dropping of entries of books past their usefulness. It is probable that we shall be able to return to printed broadsides for this special purpose, though the card catalogue in its present form may not go out of use for the index of authors, titles and subjects.

Smaller libraries will confine themselves to keeping up small working collections, chiefly of the more recent books, constantly relieved of the burden of dead books, and carefully indexed. Historical material will be confined in them to the best books on the subject at large and to a very small portion of the local field. The *omnium gatherum* historical method now advocated for the libraries of small communities and practiced by many of them, will have to be abandoned. Material will, by this method, soon accumulate beyond all possible control, and, being uncontrolled, will be of no use. Historical libraries will have to struggle with this problem of over-much material. Somehow the selective process even here must be put in operation. The libraries of a few great cities can, and probably will, go on accumulating at large for some years to come. It is well that they should. A wise winnowing process can here be discovered only by much practice on large masses of material. But before long they too will find that a book is not a book if there is nothing useful in it; and that it is better to have the best well in hand, than a mixed mass of live and dead, unorganized, material.

As President Eliot has said, the problem of housing and indexing is already a serious one at Harvard. It is not less serious in other large libraries, although the fact is not often admitted.

The plan suggested at Cambridge and Boston is one of the possible solutions of this problem of storage. This is, to erect in some place outside the city, where land is not valuable, an enormous warehouse, fireproof, simple, inexpensive, capable of indefinite extension; and to consign to it the dead volumes from all the great libraries of the region. A difficulty here arises which has already been mentioned, that of so treating the catalogues of each library contributing to this warehouse that they will show that the books removed are no longer in the library proper, but in the warehouse. This difficulty is one which, under present methods, will grow greater with each succeeding year, as the catalogues of each library increase in size and complexity. Another problem is, how to arrange the books in the warehouse so that any given volume can be found after it has been learned from the catalogues in any of the contributing libraries, that it is actually "in storage." If the coming flood is as great as it promises to be, and if ways of making, handling, storing, revising and consulting card or other catalogues, much less expensive of time, space and material than those now in use are not found, it will perhaps be necessary to cast aside all records of the books which have been pronounced dead and relegated to the storage warehouse, and treat those thus stored in the simplest possible manner—which is, to arrange them in one alphabetical series by authors. This method would discover duplicates; could be carried out by inexpensive labor; and yet would leave the books accessible to the occasional inquirer with little loss of time. The libraries proper, the efficient institutions of President Eliot's desire and President Harper's prophecy, would find themselves relieved of a tremendous burden by adopting this selective process. They could soon become far more helpful to the ordinary student than they can hope to become as long as they are struggling under the weight of books rarely used and of unwieldy catalogues.

The method of administration of the active, up to date, clean-cut working library of the future is still somewhat in question.

This working library of the future, so far as we can foretell its character, is in a building which is well-lighted and can be easily readjusted, rearranged and extended to meet new conditions. Space for readers as well as books is ample. Its stack or storeroom is planned to hold the least used books. It keeps its main working collection together, not scattering it in branches in public libraries, or in department buildings in university libraries. Branch or departmental libraries will duplicate or supplement the main library, not divide it. It is a working library, not a museum of antiquities, curios or art, and it does not invite the sight-seer. It is kept up to date, as well by weeding out of volumes past their usefulness as by the purchase of the latest publications. The most used books are most easily accessible and most fully catalogued. The latest reference lists and bibliographies on all subjects which the collection covers, are provided. Titles for purchase are selected with great care; utility, and immediate utility, being considered first, rarity, beauty and prospective value last. Rules and regulations are few and flexible. That the books be used is considered of the first importance. Museum pieces of whatever kind are not admitted to the library proper, have no place in it, and hence give no occasion for close guardianship of the shelves.

Card indexes to the proceedings of societies, to scientific journals and other publications are now being made and published. One which covers the field of zoology, published in Zurich, Switzerland, already contains over 60,000 cards. These indexes are expensive. To their first cost has to be added the cost of keeping and of the addition of new titles as they are received. In the future few libraries will find it possible to buy and keep up more than a careful selection of such lists, only those adapted to their own peculiar needs. The burden they will become in a few years will be clearly recognized. Also, the ease with which the knowledge they can impart can be transmitted from one library to another will be more fully appreciated. In this matter, as in book-buying and book-weeding, cooperation between libraries by inter-library loans will make it easier for each community to see the advantages of specialization, and of small collections kept well in hand.

The free public library of to-day does not occupy the field of book-lending as completely as it supposed it did, even a few months ago. The Book-lovers' Library has demonstrated that many people in every community will borrow books of certain classes, even at some personal expense, if the opportunity is favorable. The free public library evidently has not been offering the favorable opportunity. It is very doubtful if it ever can, or should. It will, in the future, concern itself less than ever with the circulation of light fiction. It will find it can use all the funds it can obtain in the promotion of reading of a more serious character, and in other work proper to it. It will reach out for the mechanic and the artisan— it has never yet had a hold on them—and will occupy itself more and more with the work of helping parents and teachers to train the young into the habit of reading good books, and into a working knowledge of books and journals of the informing kind.

By cooperative effort, among libraries, as illustrated by the work Mr. George Iles is doing and has done, most books as soon as published, will be evaluated at the hands of experts. The critical and expository notes thus obtained will be made generally available. Less weight will be given to the completeness of bibliographies and more to their annotations, and the skill they show in selection. Save for the maker of bibliographies, who has completeness for his only aim, a complete unannotated bibliography is of very little use.

LIBRARIES

In book selecting, in narrowing his library's field, in the casting out of dead stock, all with the help of expert advice, the librarian must be arbitrary. But in the use of the books by the public in a public library, by the students in a college library—here he will remove all barriers. The simplest and most flexible rules, based on the facts that the public owns its own institutions, and that most men are honest and considerate of one another, will enable him to see that all claims are treated alike. Suggestions, criticisms, advice, demands, will be invited from all. Public officers are public servants, and public institutions are supported to satisfy the public's needs— these good old maxims will be kept always in mind.

Librarians have passed through the repository stage, when they did little more than collect and save; the identification stage, when they devoted themselves greatly to classifying, ticketing and cataloging their books; the memorial stage—which we are unhappily still blundering through—when they surrendered themselves to the task of erecting Greek temples, Italian palaces and composite tombs; the distribution stage, wherein they find themselves outstripped by commercial ventures which saw that the novel had become as much desired as the daily paper; and they are just entering upon the critical, evaluating and educating stage. They are just beginning to find themselves, as President Harper's words testify. In this present stage they discover that they are, or may become, the center of many of the forces in their respective communities which make for social efficiency and civic improvement. The modern public library is the helpful friend of scientific, art, and historical societies; of the educational labor organizations; of city improvement organizations; of teachers' clubs and parents' societies and women's clubs. At the library should be the books and journals to which all these institutions must come for their guidance or material. Here should be rooms suitable for their gatherings. Here should be a spirit hospitable to them all; knowing what is in books, but keenly alive also to all that is best, all that is striving for helpful expression, in the people who own those books and hope much from them.

THE PLACE OF THE PUBLIC LIBRARY IN A CITY'S LIFE

*Address at the Dedication of the Trenton, N. J.,
Public Library, June 9, 1902*

Cities and towns are now for the first time, and chiefly in this country, erecting altars to the gods of good fellowship, joy, and learning. These altars are our public libraries. We had, long ago, our buildings of city and state, our halls of legislation, our courts of justice. But these all speak more or less of wrong-doing, of justice and injustice, of repression. Most of them touch closely on partisanship and bitterness of feeling. We have had, since many centuries, in all our cities, the many meeting places of religious sects—our chapels, churches and cathedrals. They stand for much that is good. But they have not brought together the communities in which they are placed. A church is not always the center of the best life of all who live within the shadow of its spire.

For several generations we have been building temples to the gods of learning and good citizenship —our schools. And they have come nearer to bringing together for the highest purpose the best impulses of all of us than have any other institutions. But they are not yet, as we hope some day they will be, for both old and young. Moreover, they speak of discipline, of master and pupil, instead only of pure and simple fellowship in studies.

And so we are, for the first time in all history, building, in our public libraries, temples of happiness and wisdom common to all. No other institution which society has brought forth is so wide in its scope; so universal in its appeal; so near to every one of us; so inviting to both young and old; so fit to teach, without arrogance, the ignorant and, without faltering, the wisest.

A public library can be the center of the activities in a city that make for social efficiency. It can do more to bind the people of a city into one civic whole, and to develop among them the feeling that they are citizens of no mean city, than any other institution yet established or than we as yet conceive.

It lends many novels. Novels are destined to play a large part in our life in the next few decades. A few hundred thousand read them now; in a few years millions will read them. As a nation, we are expressing ourselves through them; in them we are putting our history, our hopes, our ideals. Many people, confined by nature and circumstances to narrow and laborious lives, will get from their novels, here distributed, refreshment, inspiration, wider views, an admirable discontent. But they should be chosen with care. There are enough of the best to fill all needs.

The clergy will find in the library the best books in theology, biblical criticism, and religion, and these books will help them to keep from their thoughts all narrowness and hardness of doctrine.

Professional men, and men of affairs, will not incline to use their library. But it can be made so inviting that not a few will find it impossible to resist the temptation to step aside from the beaten track of the day's routine and the morning paper into some by-path of literature, science, or art.

Public libraries have not been very successful in their attempts to persuade workingmen, mechanics, artisans, to give over the sinful habit of not using their books. Perhaps it is impossible to establish the reading habit in those adults who get physically weary every day. Perhaps here we must wait for the new generation to come on with the habit ready formed, and formed largely through the influence of the library. But the library will give the opportunity. We boast of our organizing skill. We owe much, very much, of our success in manufacture and trade to our skill in uniting man to man, and men to men, in great organizations working to one common end. Much of this skill is due to a constant practice which goes with our social life. We are daily taught to cooperate. It would be difficult to find the citizen, no matter how humble his station, who does not belong to several organized bodies, who does not get from those bodies practice in working in harmony with others to effect some wished-for end. Churches, church societies, fraternal orders, social clubs, labor organizations—their name is legion. They are one of our best schools for citizenship. They help us to pick out our leaders; they teach those leaders the art of management; they teach the rank and file the profits of cooperation. And especially strong is this form of social life among the skilled craftsmen. And so a library, having the books to which it wishes to attract these men, and having rooms well fitted for their meetings, will encourage them to gather in these rooms for all the purposes that one can plainly say are non-political, are not anti-social, are educational. There is always a little barrier between the brain-worker and the hand-worker. It should be slight. It should not lead to misunderstandings. If the hand-workers discover that the library is their building and that in it they have a meeting ground common with them to all their

71

fellow-citizens, this will do much to promote good understanding and mutual good will. Of course with this use of a library go such lectures and exhibitions under the library's management as experience shows will produce good results.

I was for many years in that land where women's clubs and women voters first greatly flourished— Colorado. I learned there what woman can do by organized effort for the broadening of her own life, for the betterment of her own city. Many public libraries owe their existence to women's efforts. They are every library's good friends. Its books and rooms should, then, be made helpful in every possible way to the women and their enterprises.

Charitable and reform and educational associations of all kinds flourish amazingly in all our cities. They are of value to those who take part in them; they grow not infrequently into institutions of great influence. They should find in the library a hearty welcome, and should help to spread and strengthen the influence of its books.

With the growth of local pride among us, organizations for the improvement of cities will increase in number and grow in strength. These a library will especially try to foster. The library may well be the focal point of all those movements which make for a cleaner, a more beautiful, a more attractive city, a city in which it is better worth one's while to pass one's days. With books and photographs and lectures and other tools, much can be done to foster such a habit of self-glorification as leads to clearer vision of the improvements a city needs and a stronger determination to secure them.

To bring thorough work into better esteem; to make a little more dignified the plain, honest work of our hands; to increase the interest in his day's labor taken by the artisan; to spread a knowledge and appreciation of good design; these, as I like to understand them, are the objects of the arts-and-crafts movement, now so widespread. To a manufacturing community this movement will be of especial value. It will lead to more and better trade and technical schools, to more practical and more effective work in drawing and art study in the public schools. It is part of that wonderful renaissance of art now taking place in this country which is so interesting and so encouraging. Of such a movement the library will be one of the natural centers. In its beginnings, especially, its resources will be of the greatest help. Out of the union of those interested in this field—architects, artists, artist-artisans, patrons of art—will grow in time the museum of art and handicraft which every manufacturing city greatly needs.

Science and history will come in for attention. Societies already in existence will find in the library help in books and other material, rooms for their gatherings, quarters for storing their collections, until that happy time when each city has, as it should, a museum of science and a home for local historical material, both carefully adapted to work with young people in cooperation with the schools.

Have I gone too far afield? I am sure not. All these things which we look forward to as part of the work which a library with a beautiful home can do, have already been done, or are in the process of doing somewhere in this country today. I am not offering you an impossible ideal. I am simply outlining what experience has already proved to be the modern American free public library's proper function.

LIBRARIES

I have purposely left to the last the pleasantest, most helping thing, work with the children. Here as elsewhere in this new and wonderful field we have much to learn of detail; but here more than in any other direction we are sure of our results. We think we are a nation of readers. We have just begun to read. I believe I could prove that the practice of using the printed page, even of the daily papers, as a means of refreshment, information or training has only just begun to take root among us. Our schools and our cheap and soon to be still cheaper journals will hasten the spread of this practice. In the adult we cannot guide it. In the youth we can, and here is where the library will show its power. As an ally of the teachers in the public schools—the most useful of all the friends a library can acquire—the right books can be put into the hands of the children at the right time. The ability to read can be broadened into the habit of reading; the habit of reading can be guided into the habit of reading the things that make for wisdom and happiness. The library should buy for this purpose many books, many times more books than it thinks it will need. This will breed here a demand for good books—which it will try the library's resources and the generosity of its friends to satisfy. And through the books, again with the teachers' aid, can be reached many thousands of parents, to whom by any other method appeal would be made in vain. And through books and teachers the library will help to implant in the minds of thousands of children that pride of place, that love of neatness, that delight in a beautiful city, which will come back in another generation in an irresistible demand for the nobler and more delectable city which all hope to see.

THE INCREASE OF THINGS TO READ

*Address Delivered before the Pennsylvania Library
Association, November 19, 1902*

Institutions are results before they are causes;
they come because they are wanted, not because they
want to come; they are formed to fill certain needs,
and the needs are felt before the institutions are
formed. Libraries help to civilize, we hope and believe; but people have a certain degree of civilization
before they bring forth libraries. Let central Africa
tomorrow acquire traveling libraries thick as a plague
of flies, and let Carnegie library buildings crown
every hill in eastern Asia, and central Africans and
eastern Asians will still be as now, aliens to our
thoughts and not friends of our firesides. First come
peace and civil cooperation; then the institutions
which cooperation begets.

This idea of universal education, from which
libraries come, is quite modern. It has developed as
have all movements which tend to break down caste
distinctions. A few of the stronger and privileged
class conceived of popular education as a good thing
at just about the time that the populace itself awoke
to find it wanted education and was strong enough
to demand it, and to get it. So education grew from
a privilege to a right, and from a right to a duty.
Meanwhile, we passed from books in chains to free
public libraries.

Now, these free public libraries, the natural products of the idea of universal education as a duty, have
like the schools and like other institutions, their own
peculiar inheritance. The marks of the days when
books were few and costly, when scholars only used

them and scholars only kept them, and when scholars were all men of mediæval learning, these marks are still plain on all our libraries. It would be interesting to trace some of our peculiarities of administration, peculiarities which mark our methods off, too much perhaps, from the ways of doing things in other fields, back to the ecclesiastical, monkish, university, learned, scholastic, exclusive, privileged days of the modern library's history.

I wish now to speak of only one factor in the library's development, a factor which much influenced library methods in early library days—the supply of things to read.

The supply of things to read has increased very remarkably in the last twenty years. Statistics on the subject are of little value back of 1880. In the census for that year and in those for 1890 and 1900 we get the bases, not for exact comparisons, but for comparisons sufficiently accurate for our illumination. These figures, after allowing for all possible errors, certainly stir the imagination and encourage prophecy. Those I shall give you relate only to this country. I am indebted for them to a bulletin of the twelfth census, by William S. Rossiter, on Printing and Publishing. I commend this bulletin to your consideration. And let me commend to you also, to be read in connection with it, a recent address of Prof. Henry E. Armstrong before the educational science section of the British Association for the Advancement of Science. It is an appeal to the educational world to face more frankly the actual facts of life, and to endeavor to use those facts more freely in the exercise of the scientific imagination.

Before quoting the figures of the increase in recent years, in the last two decades, of the supply of things to read, I wish to call your attention to a few of the changes and discoveries and inventions which have helped to make this increase so great.

In 1870 a poor quality of printing paper cost 16 cents a pound. Paper of better quality is sold to-day for 2 cents a pound. A curious fact illustrative of modern newspaper methods is here worth noting. Some newspapers find that when their circulation passes a certain point the quantity of paper used each day is so great that it is difficult to supply all the copies the market demands, and at the same time keep the charges for advertising down to a rate their customers are willing or able to pay. A certain New York paper is said to have found that the cost per line of advertising in one day's issue, simply for the paper on which that line alone is printed, is 21 cents. Under present conditions a paper may almost have a circulation too large to be profitable.

Up to 1880 type was made and set very much as it had been from its first invention several hundred years before. Now the punches, one of the most expensive of the things required in type-making, are cut almost automatically from one model for type of any size of a given style. The Wicks type-casting machine is reported as about to reduce the cost of type one-half. Using this machine the London Times is set in new type every day. Certain typesetting machines do the work of several men. The Lanston monotype casts and sets and justifies lines—does all that a hand compositor can do—automatically and with astonishing rapidity, under the guidance of a strip of paper properly perforated by a machine almost as easy to operate as a typewriter. The Linotype machine casts solid bars of type with almost any desired changes of face.

All large papers and most books are stereotyped before printing. A machine now makes the stereotype plates in a fraction of a minute from a matrix formed in a few seconds. Twenty years ago the making of these plates was a slow and laborious process. The cylinder perfecting press dates back fifty years. But improvements in presses have been very marked in the past twenty. Presses are now obtainable which will deliver in one hour 100,000 newspapers complete and folded and printed in twelve colors.

I don't need to speak of recent progress in the art of newsgathering. Your daily paper tells you of it. And the syndicating method of these days whereby a score of papers have, each for a small sum, the work of the best experts in literature, science, art and other fields—this is a marvel of yesterday, yet is familiar to us all.

Books are set and stereotyped and printed as are the daily papers, and many of them almost as rapidly and cheaply. Machines fold them, gather them and sew them; machines make their covers; machines put cover and book together. A neat and attractive book bound in cloth and nicely lettered can be bought today, at retail, for 5 cents.

The advertising habit has grown. The income of newspapers in this country from advertising alone is estimated at $100,000,000 per year. This is more than double the income from the same source in 1880. The income from advertising is what makes the great newspaper possible.

While these things have been thus developing, making things to read much easier to produce and therefore much cheaper, the market for them has steadily grown. The horizon of every man is wider than it was twenty years ago; he wants to know more about things; the schools turn out more readers than ever before; every street car invites to practice in reading; every vacant lot bears on its awful front a child's first reader, and on every wayside fence from here to the Pacific is a better reading lesson than our great grandsires found in the horn-books they treasured with such care.

And what has resulted from these changes in the methods of producing things to read? In this country libraries of 1,000 volumes and over have increased in number from about 2,500 to about 5,000 in the past twenty years. The number of volumes in these libraries increased in the same period from about 12,000,000 to about 44,000,000. The new books produced each year number about 6,000. Of the copies of old books the number is outside the realm of surmise. Since 1880 the department store has come into the field. It sells books by the cord, not by the volume.

Book production to-day in this country is certainly many times what it was twenty years ago. Librarians lend a good many books in a year; for a modest guess let us say 100,000,000. But that forms only a drop in the total of the reading done in this country of the total even of the reading of books.

Of the production and reading of periodicals we must speak also chiefly in general terms, though we have a few figures which, as I have suggested, illuminate our generalities. In this country there is printed a daily newspaper every day for every five persons, about 20,000,000 copies per day. Since 1890 the capital invested in the printing and publishing business has more than doubled. In ten years the number of copies of papers and journals produced in a year has doubled. In ten years the number of copies of papers and journals produced in a year has doubled from 4,000,000,000 to 8,000,000,000. In fifty years the same product has increased twenty fold. Mr. Rossiter tells me he got these figures from returns sent into the census office direct from the publishers. I worked out the same statistics two years ago from a newspaper directory. My totals were about half as large as those of the twelfth census. The truth probably lies somewhere between the two. Of this total issue the daily papers form about two-thirds. Other kinds of publications have increased much more slowly than the newspapers. The latter are gradually taking up the whole field. They will increase in number. They have not yet secured as readers, so I believe, more than one-fourth of the total of possible readers in this country, which I put at about 40,000,000. These 30,000,000 non-consumers of to-day will come into the reading class with tremendous rapidity. Progress in such matters, as George Iles so aptly says, is by leaps and bounds. The newspaper reader is a possible book reader. In many cases he becomes both a book reader and a book buyer. The book market will increase in the next twenty years as it never has before—even in the astonishing last two decades of the nineteenth century. With a greater market there will come a relative decrease in the price per volume. The prizes of authorship will increase, more will write, and if our entire civilization is not moving on the wrong road, books will be better as well as cheaper and greater in number.

In a country which is rushing headlong into the printing, publishing and reading habits; with the production of things to read, from the most trivial journal to the most ponderous volume of science or history, all on a purely commercial basis, what is the work we are to do? We were once keepers of the books; now we are keepers of a few of the many millions of books. Books were once the greater part of all that there was to read; now books are but a trifling portion of the things that are daily read.

We must learn to handle books with less labor and expense. Our incomes cannot, in their growth, keep pace with the growth in the number of the books we must take care of. The new book in very many cases deprives the older book of its usefulness. We must find some way of dropping from shelves and our lists the older books which age makes useless. A distinction is made between books of power and books of knowledge. The conclusions drawn from this classification do not hold, save in small degree. The distinction is even very misleading in some of the aspects under which it has been presented. There are great old books, which are broad, universal, enduring, because they give us the penetrating view of life of the man of genius, of the seer, the poet, the native-born psychologist. There are others which have gathered greatness with the lapse of time because a fashion of scholarship, the dictates of a religion, the literary customs of a people have led to their retention, and have woven them by quotation, paraphrase and allusion into the fabric of present literature. But these books are not many. A great part of those which are often counted as among them simply shine by a little borrowed light. And the best of the books of power—the worship which comes to them is often born of a fashion, of a pseudo culture which apes the real thing. And as the newspaper comes still closer to life, takes all knowledge for its province still more fully, brings us in closer touch each day with other peoples and their civilizations, we must—at least the coming generation must—loosen a little our hold on the historic, mythologic, religious and literary background of our own people that we may have time and strength and brain to spare for the task of broadening into a sympathetic understanding of those other peoples. What Darwin lays down as the foundation of social order, sympathy, has, for indispensable elements, community of interest and likeness in knowledge. We hope for the federation of the world. In preparation for it each race must regard less exclusively its own past and acquaint itself more freely and more willingly with the religious and social legacies of other races. So the great books will lose their uniqueness, because other great books of other great peoples will stand beside them as their equals.

Moreover, it is not from books, even from the great books, that the man of action chiefly gets his insight into human nature, into the society in which he lives. Life is before him. He sees it, lives it, and interprets it for himself. The thing he needs, that he may first exercise his imagination on the work that lies before him, and then carry out that which he has imagined, is the latest record of man's control over nature. His psychology comes from birth and daily exercise. His facts, these must be handed to him by his fellows. It is science that he must have. The books of chemistry, of engineering, of machinery —these are for him the books of power. The great books of the humanities, these we must have; but with these, almost before these, we must have the books of knowledge.

And they come, and go, so swiftly; they replace one another like shadows on the wall. Those which time has made useless gather on our shelves; old age and desuetude creep on them almost in a day. We must drop the old ones; secure the new ones; make them quickly accessible; invite all to their use; gather young workingmen about them; make ourselves in this field of action—this field which covers so great a part of the whole area of modern life—quite indispensable.

To come to simple and practicable suggestions: we librarians should collect and publish in various forms annotated lists of the latest books as they appear on scientific and industrial subjects. We are several thousand strong. We can cooperate if we will. We should not wait for men outside our ranks again to set us the example.

Open shelves are here to stay. The public knows when it comes into its own, even if it does not always know its own before it inherits it. A business institution can place its books on open cases in a thousand drug stores and count its losses as a small fraction of what it gains thereby. Why cannot the public library bring its books in somewhat similar fashion into the heart of a city, and count the gain to 999 citizens as more than compensating for their loss from the meanness of the thousandth.

I wonder if publicity of scandals promotes wickedness? Vice stalks at large through a thousand thousand pages of the public press each day. I wonder if thereby vice grows in favor? Probably more crimes are read of every day in America by more people than in any other country in the world. I wonder if we are more vicious than others? I doubt it. At any rate it waits to be proved. Of the viceful novel the same things are true. We read them; and our social fabric still hangs together. My conclusion is this, that, as to fiction in our libraries it is simplemindedness in us that leads us to haggle and quibble over the question of admitting a certain novel to our shelves when the papers every day give everybody their full of stories more immoral than the novel and when the very novel in question has, while we weigh and consider, already been read by more thousands than will ever find it on our shelves. I am aware that as a public institution we must lend an ear to Mrs. Grundy —I would it were a deaf one! But with fiction, the question is not so much, does it square with our notions of purity, as has it strength? Is it alive? Is it true? Does it say something? Is it from the brain of a prophet, a poet, a diviner of things? The canting twaddler, his are the books we can dispense with.

I would like to speak of the opportunities libraries have, from the changed conditions of printing and of picture reproduction, to promote the best kind of art education—the art education which means increased art appreciation, increased æsthetic sensitiveness. But that is too long a story. I must, however, call your attention, though very briefly, to the work that lies before us in cooperation with publishers and book sellers. Our present controversy with them is deplorable. It is born of ignorance of the mutual aid we might give one another, the possibility of which seems never to have been realized. To mention only one point: above all other persons we hold the key to the tastes and interests, as to the books for young people in this country—the coming readers and buyers of books. This through our intimate and friendly relations with schools and teachers. In one way and another I have from time to time in the past ten years tried to tell publishers that libraries can help them, and would like to do so, and I have tried to tell librarians that they can help the publishers, and that they should. The publishers have stood by the conservatism of the dollars in sight; we have stood on a stupid dignity, and we are apparently farther apart than ever. I believe that the full and free discussion of our relations, which is coming, will result in our arriving at an understanding of one another and at a generous and helpful cooperation.

Another point in our management of libraries illuminated by a plain presentation of the facts of modern print-production is our relations to the daily press. The press must and does give us the "news." Within this little word are now embraced all aspects of human activity. Our function it will be to help the people who establish us to select from all printed presentments of the life of today those best adapted to their needs. From the papers we can rightly ask, and, save for slips now and then, due to human frailties, to weak points unavoidable in a machine so great and complex as a modern newspaper office, we need never ask in vain for sympathetic aid. We have never asked enough. A body of workers as large as ours, one not lacking in persons of sense and discernment, engaged heart and soul in a good and helpful public service, a body like this owes it to the work it is trying to do to put that work early, late and often before the public. I have long advocated a committee of the American Library Association on publicity. It should have taken up the work ten years ago. It is not too soon to begin. Our forerunners were students, consumers of the midnight oil. They held themselves apart. They modestly offered to the world, now and again, the results of their labors. Our work is different; we make libraries useful to the scholars, but also we try to make them active agencies in popular education. For this latter work especially we need daily the publicity, the kindly criticism and the encouragement which the newspapers have always shown themselves ready to give.

MERE WORDS

Address Delivered before the New Jersey State Teachers' Association, Trenton, December 29, 1902

We sometimes speak scornfully of "mere words." That is because it is easier to make sounds than it is to talk sense. Orators tend to run to sound. A pinch of plain reason makes a multitude of fine words seem like substantial mental food. The younger we are the more ready we are to take the crackling of a few thorns for a good hot fire. Where deception is easy deceivers multiply. So good teachers are always on the watch against the word habit. And they wisely speak in scorn, sometimes, of "mere words."

But now and then the word's side of the case may properly be presented.

Words mark us off from other animals. When we had invented language we had climbed on to the high table-land of humanity. We are the only reasonable race. If other creatures are rational, their reasoning is hardly of our kind. We think almost solely in words; and can we think of a thought which —not using words—is not the kind of thought we use when we think? The question is a pleasant puzzle. At least it serves my turn, for I am trying to bring up vividly the idea that words underlie our whole life; are the signs of our nobility and a cause thereof; are bonds of society, the records of our progress and the steps on which we rise. And they are, some of them, as full of emotion as others are of meaning. Association, constant use, experience, story, fable, history, all have made them able to arouse in us sentiments grave and gay, feelings of grief, pity, joy, reverence, emotion, wonder. It is a curious and astounding thing this power to touch all the stops in the complex organ of our emotions which a "mere word" enjoys. Were a violinist to play to you here and now a bar or two from "Yankee Doodle" or "America" or "Home, Sweet Home" or "Dixie," you would be moved, each and every one of you; vaguely perhaps, perhaps very definitely, but somehow the mere vibration of the strings of the violin would thrill through every one of us. This is wonderful when soberly thought of. Still more wonderful it is that the vibrations I may set in motion from my throat, fashioned at my will to make a certain familiar word, can likewise move you, and still more definitely, deeply, and permanently than the far more cunningly-fashioned notes of the violin. I will try it. Be as coldly observant and critical as you please —while I simply name to you a few names—it will only make my little experiment the more interesting:

"Aladdin, Babylon, the Pyramids, Homer, Ulysses, the Parthenon, the Tiber, Julius Caesar, the Goths, Charlemagne, King Alfred, Richard of the Lion Heart, the Crusades, Napoleon, Waterloo, Lexington, Washington, the Nile, Pharaoh, Moses, Palestine, Herod, the sea of Galilee, Nazareth, the Garden of Gethsemane, Calvary."

As I repeated those words you got from them a feeling of sympathy, of awe, of vast distance, of long lapse of years, of exultation, of reverence, of tenderness, and with these feelings, not at once perhaps as strong and clear as "Dixie" could arouse, but deeper, came a tumult of thoughts of every form and nature. In, or with, or by those few simple sounds you traveled, from the Egypt of three thousand years ago down through Greece and Rome, and the Middle Ages,

and modern times to our Revolution, and then went
back for a moment to the great figure of all history
and to the religion in which you live. Just a handful
of words. Consider their power. "Mere words!"
This is not all of my argument. This sensitiveness to words does not come by nature. One may
be born to be musical. One is not born to a knowledge of Julius Caesar. We speak of such things as
my little list of words recalls as part of the inheritance of the race. They are not so save in a re-
stricted sense. We do not inherit them. We learn
them. Many times as the story of Aladdin has been
told, it must be told again for each and every child,
as new generations come on the stage. Consider the
observation, reading, and study that each of you
engaged in before your brains were so attuned that
those simple sounds I made aroused in them sympathetic vibrations of thought and feeling. Was it
worth your while? Do you feel that, being thus
attuned, you have a better claim to rank as women of
intelligence?

We all seek pleasure. To make to-morrow not less
full of joy than to-day, and to keep from it some of
to-day's pains and sorrows; this sums up our aims. I
am not forgetting that one of to-morrow's anticipated
pleasures may be the making others a little happier
than we did to-day. I am not now going into the
field of ethics. I am trying to bring out in a little
different light the old picture of the delights of a
many-sided interest. The oyster may find content in
mud and high water, the cow in her cud and the shade
of a tree. We of the great race of human-kind have
long thought it better worth our while to count time
by interests, images, thoughts, emotions, than by vacations and holidays. We like to live. We think living

is worth while. And we put all we can into the
field of our own intellect and emotions, that life may
thereby be long, however short and few its days.

Going on with the argument for a moment: far
more effective in playing on our emotions and broadening our horizon than single words, are words in
combination. Here the skill of the artist comes in,
and here, too, we get in greater strength the elements
of memory, habit, association, and suggestion. This
is a commonplace, the power of language; our dependence on it; the strong and many-stranded and
multi-colored warp it makes for the wonderful tapes-
try of the life of man, of which our daily conduct is
the woof.

It is a commonplace, but one that we find more
marvelous, more admirable, fresher in its newness
with each day's progress in our lifelong education.

Let me point my moral with a few simple phrases
which your own manner of up-bringing have made fit
to move you:

"In the beginning God created the heaven and the
earth.

"And the earth was without form, and void; and
darkness was upon the face of the deep; and the
Spirit of God moved upon the waters. And God
said, Let there be light: and there was light.

*   *   *   *   *   *   *

"Then the Lord answered Job out of the whirlwind,
and said:

"Who is this that darkeneth counsel by words,
without knowledge?

"Gird up now thy loins like a man; for I will
demand of thee and answer thou me.

"Where wast thou when I laid the foundations of
the earth? declare, if thou hast understanding.

MERE WORDS

"Who hath laid the measures thereof, if thou knowest: or who hath stretched the line upon it?

"Whereupon are the foundations thereof fastened? or who laid the corner thereof;

"When the morning stars sang together, and all the sons of God shouted for joy?

*   *   *   *   *   *   *

"Canst thou bind the sweet influence of Pleiades, or loose the bands of Orion?

"Canst thou bring forth Mazzaroth in his season; or canst thou guide Arcturus with his sons?

"Knowest thou the ordinances of heaven? Canst thou set the dominion thereof in the earth?

*   *   *   *   *   *   *

"The Lord is my Shepherd; I shall not want.

"He maketh me to lie down in green pastures: he leadeth me beside the still waters.

"He restoreth my soul: he leadeth me in the paths of righteousness for his name's sake.

"Yea, though I walk through the valley of the shadow of death, I will fear no evil: for thou art with me; thy rod and thy staff they comfort me."

*   *   *   *   *   *   *

Of the power of these phrases to move us I need not speak. We read them, we hear them—and they conquer us.

We have come now to reading, and I am nearer the point I wish to impress upon you. I have reminded you that you live in words; that through them your life is compact of meaning and full of delights. I have needed but to hint that only by long study, by constant practice in them, by varied experience with thousands of them in many thousands of relations, have words come to bring to you a full burden of suggestion, a good measure of joy.

91

The conclusion is plain. To live a full life we must win a full appreciation of all that words convey, we must understand their simplest message; also, we must feel their deeper significance, as when a master hand plays upon them and presents to us—as does Emerson, for example, in his "Concord Bridge"—a world of human nature and human life in a few short lines.

This is no question of A, B, C. This knowledge of words does not come at the end of the Fourth Reader. This is a matter of many men of talents as set forth in their books. To know life, to feel life, to know our fellows, to live, in a deep sense of that word, we must have met the kings among men in the words in which they have set themselves before us. The old things that belong to our race, the gods, the heroes, the scenes, the deeds, the fancies of our fathers' fathers, all these we must have taken up into ourselves before life can have for us that fullness we desire. In a word, we must read.

We have come now to the relations of libraries and schools. The libraries are established that they may gather together the best of the fruits of the tree of human speech, spread them before men in all liberality and invite all to enjoy them. The schools are in part established that they may tell the young how to enjoy this feast. They do this. How much more they do for civility, honesty, and other simple and fundamental virtues in those first six years of school I am not here to tell you. They teach the young to read. They put them in touch with words and phrases; they point out to them the delectable mountains of human thought and action as set forth in "mere words," and then they let them go. It is to be lamented that they go so soon. At twelve, at thirteen, at fourteen at the most these young men and women in your care, whose lives could be so broadened, sweetened, mellowed, humanized by a few years' daily contact with the wisest, noblest, wittiest of our kind as their own words portray them—at this early age, when reading has hardly begun, they leave you, and they leave almost all of the best reading at the same time. If, now—and I told you my point is an old, familiar one, of which, none the less, I hope you will never tire—if now, you can bring these young citizens of yours into sympathy with the books the libraries would persuade them to read; if you make "mere words" inviting to them; if you can impress upon them the reading habit; then the libraries can supplement your good work; will rejoice in empty shelves; will feel that they are not in vain; and the coming generations will delight, one and all, in that which good books can give; will speak more plainly; will think more clearly; will be less often led astray by the "mere words" of false prophets of every kind; will see that all men are of the one country of humanity; and will, to sum it all, be better citizens of a good state.

To get children into the reading habit you need right at your elbow some of the good books the libraries contain. You need this one to help you in your work; that one to broaden, for the pupils, the text book's limited view; another to tell them more of the great man or the notable event at which the lesson only hints. You need them to help you to find the one field of knowledge in which that boy, a seeming monument of indifference—and you all have such in your classes—may find an interest; and always you need them of many kinds to promote practice in reading, to encourage the reading habit, to send home with the pupils to their firesides.

The day will come when every schoolroom in the

land will be a branch of its nearest library. All present tendencies in library work point that way. That is the relation of library and school I have worked towards for a good many years. Children must learn to read. They must learn to read readily, and to read understandingly. For this they need practice. They must form the habit of reading; and the habit of reading good things. And all this they must do before they leave your care at thirteen or fourteen years of age. The supplementary reader has done much in this direction. How much only the older among you can realize. The libraries, with a branch in every schoolroom, will do more. What can you do to help them?

First, if you have a public library in your town make yourself familiar with it. Learn how to use it; how to get books from it; learn to use its books of reference, what its resources are in the lines you are teaching, and discover all the things it is willing and able to do for you in the way of books. Will it lend you an armful? Will it buy the books you ask for, if not already on its shelves? Will it welcome your pupils and lend them books? Will it receive courteously a roomful of them if they come for some reasonable purpose? Learn those things. You will find the learning a pleasure.

Next, test your own knowledge of the best books for the young. If you have not read them already, if evil fortune denied to your childhood the fearsome delight of discovering, with Crusoe, a strange footprint on the sandy shore; if you never saw Giant Despair overthrown, or the Sleeping Beauty wake, or the portcullis graze Marmion's plume, it is still not too late. You sinned, or were sinned against, or both. But the gateway to the realm of childhood's

94

fancies is never closed. Get Scudder's "Children's Book" and read it through.

Read also the good books about children by grown up people for grown up people. Try Barrie's "Little White Bird," and see if birth and education have made you fit to enjoy a master of English, a man of tenderest sympathies, a prophet of the land of children.

All this, you may tell me you have done. This seems to you an old story. Your supplementary readers have brought you and your pupils into close touch with these things. Let us hope this is so.

But I believe you will find there is something yet to do in reading in which the library can be of help. Reading comes by practice. The practice which a pupil gets during school hours does not make him a quick and skillful reader. There is not enough of it. If you encourage the reading habit and lead that habit, as you easily can, along good lines, your pupils will gain much, simply in knowledge of words, in ability to get the meaning out of print, even though we say nothing of the help their reading will give them in other ways.

I have lectured you enough. I am afraid I may alarm you by my preaching; may make books seem a burden and public libraries things to be avoided. That would be a grievous mistake. Libraries are pleasant places. Their shelves do not groan with the wisdom that is on them. They delight in their burdens. Their books are like your own companions, grave or gay, as nature made them. And one may believe that the great men, our fellows, who made the best of them, rejoice mightily when any words of theirs add to the happiness of any one of us.

Libraries are founded to add to the joy of your lives and to lighten your daily work.

95

FICTION-READERS AND LIBRARIES

Outlook, June 27, 1903

Some observers of the book market believe the day of the booming of the novel is nearly over. They think that the time when a new story can be puffed and advertised into tremendous popularity is past. This opinion has little basis in fact. Novels have been increasingly with us for a round hundred years. For several thousand years men have taken pleasure in prose fiction. Like the ruler, the priest, the trader, and the artist, the story-teller has been with us from camp-fires to cities and from huts to palaces. We cannot shake him off, and would not if we could. He has made us known to ourselves. At his best he has interpreted life for us, broadened us and mellowed us; at his poorest he has diverted us and made us forget the pettiness of our work and spirit. When his tales found the opportunity of print, and multiplied themselves a thousand times in an hour, his fascination did not increase, but his circle of listeners widened. It is widening still.

Consider the present situation and its signs of the future. There are to-day in this country probably twice as many readers of newspapers as there were ten years ago. Many of those who read before now read more. But those who read ten years ago could not, if they read all day and all night, consume the thousands of millions of papers and journals our presses now give us each year. The ranks of the readers get new recruits every day. A few come up into the reading class through high schools and colleges; but only the smallest fraction through the latter, and only a pitifully small percentage through the former. The most come up through A, B, ab, street signs, posters, nickel stories, and the daily paper itself.

Not all of us are readers yet. There is much popular error on this subject. Few adults in America are illiterates; but not all who know how to read take advantage of their knowledge. The majority of all the possible readers in this country do not, properly speaking, read at all. I mean this literally. I do not mean that they do not clearly understand what they read, but that they do not use print, save very rarely, for any purpose whatsoever. But out of this majority there are passing every year thousands and tens of thousands into the reading class. That this change has been taking place rapidly in the past ten years the growth of newspaper production and of an accompanying newspaper consumption in that period is abundant evidence. That the transformation is not complete, that many millions of literates have yet to graduate into the class of actual readers, could be shown by statistics of present newspaper consumption and of the possible readers in the country, set forth in connection with a study of the areas in which the present output of reading is consumed. Every month and every year a new army of users of print marches into the field out of the country of the non-reading. This army is recruited partly from the additions to our population, but chiefly, as I have said, from those who could read before and did not. These incoming hordes of devourers of books are nearly all of the class that gets its fundamentals only from the public schools, its practice from wayside fences and daily papers. They want the facts of life. They get them, disjointed and disconnected, from the newspapers. They want also the story; the romance;

the continuous, connected narrative, reflecting their own life, but touched with more emotion than they are quite conscious of, and painting their ideals in bright, unmistakable colors with broad, strong contrasts. In a word, they want stories. At first they read chiefly authors whose names never appear in our literary journals. They read them more than any save careful observers ever realize. Gradually, out of the many millions, a few millions come into the field which we complacently speak of as "current literature." And these few millions are they who make it sure that novels, as they appear in this field of current literature, will continue to sell in huge editions, and will continue to be as readily subject to booms by skillful advertising as the latest soap or the newest health food. The sum of it all is, the people, as always, want stories.

And stories are probably good for them. The novel today seems to express the present man more fully than any other form of literature. It is the most common form of art. It can touch all subjects, express all feelings, teach all doctrines. Unless all signs fail, it is sure to widen its field still further, to become still more widely read, to teach us more readily, to set forth our character, history, and aims more comprehensively still.

As a librarian the subject of novels interests me keenly. The librarian is a public servant, appointed primarily not as a censor but as a distributer of books. He is employed to supply, but within certain limits, the books the people ask for. What are the limits? The people wish novels; novels are probably helpful to them—which novels shall he give them?

Financial considerations compel a selection. No library can buy all. Help in finding an approximate answer to this important question can be got by learning which authors, by the libraries' own showing, are chiefly in demand to-day.

From thirty-four typical libraries in this country —libraries ranging in size from those of New England country towns to those of cities like St. Louis and Cleveland—I obtained lists of the names of all the authors of fiction for adults represented by the novels lent on three separate days; also figures showing the total number of books of each author lent on the three days. These names and figures I have tabulated, and I give some of the more important results below.

In reading the names and figures several things should be taken note of, if we would avoid an entire misunderstanding of them. In the first place, this list shows the preference, not of book-buyers, but of free public library users. Of course borrowers at public libraries are also buyers of books, but this list represents their preferences as borrowers. General observation permits us to conclude that it represents fairly well also the preferences of the borrowers, and others, as book-buyers. The "best-selling" novels of a given week are usually the most often-asked-for novels at the public libraries. This list, however, fails to follow the best-selling list more closely than it does because not all libraries buy all the best-selling novels, and because the borrower at the library usually takes some novel, even if he cannot get the novel of his choice; and because this list, being a list of authors, not of books, is affected greatly by the fact that some of the authors in it are represented in most libraries by many different titles. Crawford, for example, stands first, partly by reason of the fact that he is almost always on the shelves. He is taken many times as a last resort. He is fairly popular; and then there are so many of him!

Then we should remember that this list represents in a measure the preference for books of a certain general class, rather than a preference for specific authors. Mary Johnston and Winston Churchill, for example, stand near the head; but they are there because their books are of the type now popular—historic, dramatic, simple, and superficial, rather than deep and elemental. Were they to publish no more books, their names would drop out of sight on another list of this kind made up a year from now; while Dumas and Dickens, men of more individuality, appealing to more permanent tastes, would occupy about the same positions they do here.

Again, this is a list of writers, not of books. Were it a list of books, we may be sure the names would be very differently arranged. Mr. Crunden, of the St. Louis Library, has shown, by careful study of the issue of the more popular of the novels on his shelves, that "Les Misérables," "Vanity Fair," "The Three Guardsmen," and other books, put by common consent among the great books of the world, are those most often read by library borrowers; that they maintain their places in the front rank, in spite of the seemingly greater popularity of the novels of the hour.

I have alluded to the fact that Crawford and other authors of like fecundity, as King and Roe, owe their prominence in part to the fact that they have written so many books. They are assisted in gaining their eminence—I am not now attempting to say whether that eminence reflects credit on the work the public libraries are doing or not—by the practice which is common in libraries of buying all the works of an author as they appear once he has gained the public's ear. It is quite customary, for example, having met the public demand with a dozen copies of the first success of Jenkins, to buy a dozen of Jenkins's later efforts as they appear, regardless of the question of their merit. And while they are doing this, librarians neglect, as inquiries I have made have shown, to supply the constant demand for the older novels on which time has set the seal of approval. Of a list of one hundred of the best novels, compiled by any competent judge, most librarians would find on their shelves in the busy season hardly more than half, in good presentable condition. This manner of novel-buying of course works to the disadvantage of the standards, and helps to bring into greater use the authors we find first on my list. But here another fact should be borne in mind—that, of popular novels of the hour no library buys enough copies to supply the demand. As it is the actual demand we are trying to measure, our figures fail us in that they show the demand as modified by an insufficient supply. If all the libraries contributing to this report were to purchase the latest popular novel up to the limit of the inquiries made for it, a list like this would change as to the authors which stand near its head almost from day to day. Probably this ever-present limit of supply gives us in these returns a better index to the character of the average reading called for than would like returns from libraries which supplied all calls for the latest craze in fiction.

To make the significance of this list and its accompanying figures perfectly plain, I should say again that in thirty-four representative libraries in this country there were lent on three days in the current year a total of 19,144 novels. These novels were by about 1,200 authors. Of the total number of novels—in round numbers, 20,000—678 were by F. Marion Crawford, 535 by Rosa N. Carey, 486 by Alexandre Dumas. Only those authors, seventy-seven in all, are here given whose books were lent to the number of more than seventy.

Novelists pleasing to the ladies are in the lead. Carey, Douglas, Amelia Barr, and Burnham are universal favorites with the women whose literary life is not unduly strenuous, who like a story of true love dealing with a manner of life not conspicuously differing from their own. These leaders in popularity, like almost all on the list, are proper, conventional, and clean, and if the common opinion about novels and novel-reading is correct, they may be said to be, with few exceptions, wholesome.

The writers of fiction whom time has tried and experience has approved of are not near the front. Of Dickens, Scott, George Eliot, Thackeray, and Hawthorne, 772 novels were read out of the total of 20,000, or less than 4 per cent.; while Carey, Douglas, Barr, Burnham, and Captain King found favor in the eyes of 2,087 borrowers, or nearly 11 per cent of all.

These figures probably represent fairly well the popular taste; that is, they represent the taste of that small portion of the community which keeps in a literary way up to the level, in general journalism, of the Ladies' Home Journal, and in current literature of The Bookman. These readers include most of the readers of such books as come rightly or by a kind courtesy into the field of "literature." Of all the readers in the country they form, as I intimated earlier in this paper, only a small part. But they include most of the managers and directors of affairs.

103

They are the substantial, socially efficient people on whom we rely. And this table here is a bit of evidence as to the wholesomeness of their tastes.

Of course, if libraries were not all censors of reading in good degree, if they did not choose to keep the most frothy and the undeniably filthy from their shelves, this would be a different showing. But with shelves thus unguarded there would come to them much more freely other elements of the community, and our list would no longer be so closely indicative of the tastes of our friends and neighbors. It would speak of tastes which we know exist, but find it possible to ignore.

List of the names of authors of fiction for adults more than seventy of whose works were borrowed in three days at thirty-four representative free public libraries in the country, with the number of copies borrowed in each case:

Rank.	Author	Vols.	Rank.	Author	Vols.
1	Crawford	678	17	Crockett	256
2	Carey	535	18	Hector (Mrs. Alexander)	253
3	Dumas	486			
4	Douglas	396	19	Ford	235
5	Barr, Amelia	391	20	Caine	226
6	Burnham	390	21	Dickens	221
7	Doyle	389	22	Wilkins	219
8	King	375	23	Mitchell	212
9	Hope	336	24	Howells	194
10	Parker	329	25	Corelli	184
11	Stockton	328	26	Bulwer	180
12	Roe	323	27	Kipling	179
13	Johnston	303	28	Davis, R. H.	173
14	Churchill	302	29	Besant	172
15	Holmes, M. J.	299	30	Green, A. K.	169
16	Burnett	261	31	Merriman	165

FICTION-READERS AND LIBRARIES

Rank.	Author	Vols.	Rank.	Author	Vols.
32	Pool	165	55	Chambers	115
33	Black	164	56	Page	113
34	Scott	162	57	Catherwood	113
35	Bacheller	162	58	Craik	112
36	Duchess, The	159	59	Hawthorne	105
37	Collins	158	60	Wood, Mrs.	104
38	Eliot	148	61	Pemberton	103
39	Cooper	146	62	Yonge	101
40	Lyall, Edna	144	63	Russell	100
41	Harte	140	64	Balzac	97
42	Marlitt	138	65	Braddon	95
43	Allen, J. L.	136	66	Harrison, Mrs.	95
44	Thackeray	136	67	Castle	93
45	Wilson, A. E.	135	68	Winter, J. S.	93
46	Barrie	134	69	Tarkington	92
47	Harland	132	70	Hardy	88
48	Thompson	131	71	Brady	87
49	Ward, Mrs.	127	72	Blackmore	85
50	Cable	124	73	Major	84
51	Stevenson	122	74	Zangwill	80
52	Reade	118	75	Kirk	79
53	Haggard	118	76	Mark Twain	77
54	Weyman	118	77	Runkle	71

WHAT THE PEOPLE READ

Outlook, December 5, 1903

Things to read and readers to enjoy them increase in ways we scarcely note, and with results none can estimate. If man is better for knowing more, then no generation has matched our own in excellence. To be informed is not the same as to be wise; but certainly it is a step away from ignorance.

Every roadside fence is now a primer for the passer-by, every trolley-car a first reader to the traveler, and every hoarding a treatise on zoölogy, manufactures, and social problems. To-day, most read a little, if only the signs and posters; some read newspapers—probably ten to twenty millions of the forty millions who could read them if they would. A few read novels; if the most popular novel finds only a million buyers in a country where forty millions could read it if they would, who can say that novel-readers are more than a few? A very few, possibly two or three millions, read standard literature and serious contributions to thought and knowledge. Surely, the procession of readers grows larger every year, relatively as well as absolutely. The change in the character of what it reads, of this much can be said, little can be proved. The penny-dreadful and the Beadle of delightful memory led the way to the nickel library and the copious chronicles of the little things of home. Alonzo and Melissa have their successors on every news-stand, and "Scottish Chiefs" still give us blissful thrills, with no change of scene or costume and with slight deference to the latest fashion in dialogue. The best poetry seems to follow old models, and, as ever, there is little of the best, and that little, little read. Gibbon wrote good history long ago; Darwin put forth the great book of science before most of us were born; and we get good histories and good science still. But now, as then, their readers are few.

In the last ten years young people have come to form a large proportion of library borrowers, taking now nearly a third of all books lent. Like their elders, the children are fond of story-books, and select them seventy-four times out of a hundred. Adults read seventy novels to thirty other books, showing an apparent increase in the popularity of the "other books" of about 40 per cent in ten years.

Some complain that our natural history runs now to sentiment, and that the sentiment is only a little less false than the natural history. Glory be to the sentimentalist none the less. The librarian now enjoys with the teacher the sight of countless thousands of children eager to learn of the joys and trials of those other children of the wild. Thus sympathy comes and interest with it, and the habits of kindness and gentleness follow after. Every public library in the land is to-day a whole Kindness-to-Animals Society in itself, through the books of nature stories on its shelves.

The geography of the schools is a far broader subject than it formerly was. The teacher now supplements the text book in a hundred ways. She calls on her public library for all that can throw light on the country under review, and travels written to attract the young are her especial delight. Yet our figures show no increase in travel reading. This awaits explanation.

Where borrowers took one hundred books on social science ten years ago they now take one hundred and ninety. This is not due to a greater interest in partisan politics, which in libraries goes chiefly with history and biography. The newspapers seem to give the people a surfeit of party platforms, issues, and candidatorial platitudes.

Of history and biography the use among adults seems not to increase; but children call for them, and have raised the total lendings in ten years by 70 and 24 per cent respectively. This is encouraging to the librarian, even though he knows he must chiefly thank his helpmeet the teacher for the change. From the historical story which the writer of boys' books weaves about Ticonderoga and Ethan Allen, to a biography of Allen and a history of the Revolution, is an easy step, under a teacher's guidance. Moreover, the child of foreign parents, still speaking his mother tongue at home, is eager to know of his new country, and calls for books of history and biography —real, true things he wants—where the American boy more often asks for stories. This phenomenon is not yet fully explained. It is observed in all libraries near centers of foreign population. It is one aspect of that astonishing assimilative power which our country possesses, and uses, almost unconsciously, to mold to its own ways all who come within its influence.

But, after all, the change in reading for the better, as library statistics demonstrate it, is rather slight. The figures seem to indicate a drift from overmuch of literature of feeling—the novel—to literature of thinking; from emotion to judgment. They suggest it only; they do not demonstrate it. Such a change cannot be expected. None the less, we may find much cause for congratulation in the present situation.

I have made a diagram illustrating the print-using

habit in the life of our people. If read from left to right, the whole area represents the whole population of the United States. Its height represents, at the extreme left, all persons living who are under one year of age, and then, passing to the right, all those of each successive age, up to seventy, as indicated by the numbers at the bottom. The heavy curved line is the line of school attendance. School begins to gather in the children when they are four; at seven it holds, for a time each year, 70 per cent of all of that age. Nearly all who enter remain until they are from ten to twelve. Then they begin to leave in large numbers, and hardly more than 30 per cent enter the high school at fourteen or fifteen, and the merest fraction enter college at nineteen or twenty. This tells the story. We scarcely do more than teach our children to read.

Between those who read much and those who read none there is of course no such hard and fast line as I have suggested. There are but few who do not read at least the signs on the street-cars or the posters by the country road. But reading, even in a very broad sense of the word, has not yet become a universal habit. Those who teach, those who read many things themselves, those who write books or contribute to newspapers, all associate chiefly with reading people. They see countless opportunities for reading thrust under the eyes of every one. They consider the newspapers, the schools, the libraries, their own children, their own associates, and they conclude that every one reads. Then they take note of the character of the print which confronts all eyes, the yellow journal, the trifling novel, the flimsy magazine, the nickel story papers, the torrent of that literature which they scorn, which rarely gets even the compliment of condemnation from even the most trivial of literary journals, the literature of the submerged 90 per cent; and, viewing all these things, they conclude that not only does every one read, but that most read wretched stuff, and that the reading public's taste steadily deteriorates. Whereas the situation in fact is this: School attendance grows steadily larger every year, relatively as well as absolutely. It includes more of the children of five and six. It gathers more of the four and five-year-olds. And especially does it hold in school more children as they come to the working ages of twelve, thirteen, and fourteen. This means that every year the million who leave school have had a longer training in print-using. At the same time, through school libraries and public libraries, and a wiser use of good literature for reading lessons, these million have each year more of the reading habit and a better taste. Most of them have, however, not passed the sixth grade. Most of them come from homes where no reading is done. Most of them go at once into fields of work where reading is not a habit and "literature" is an unknown word. And to these we must add the many thousands who do not pass through the school area at all, not even for a few short years. We have, then, coming to-day into this vast kingdom of print—so appallingly vast, so depressingly commonplace—a procession with the same general characteristics it has long had: a handful of college graduates, a larger group of high school graduates—combined, not 10 per cent of the whole—and a rank and file which reads very little, and that with difficulty. The procession, I say, has the same characteristics it has had for several generations past; but it is larger, vastly larger, and grows larger every year. The demand for something to read comes now

111

from millions, formerly from a few thousand. They demand reading suited to their capacities and tastes, and the supply comes forth. The bill-board, the penny paper, and the 5-cent dreadful, these are their third and fourth readers, their literary primers, their introductions to better things. In reading them they are teaching themselves and improving themselves, and in almost the best possible way. They get what they wish, they read with interest and pleasure, they

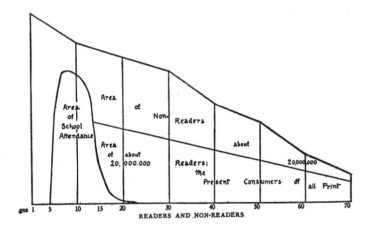

take profit therefrom. Moreover—and this is the other weighty fact in the case—they steadily improve in their choice. The chronicle of the growth of clean and wholesome journals, daily, weekly, and monthly, in the past two decades is just as wonderful in its way as that of the growth of those yellow papers which make us cringe.

Cheap and loud newspapers will go on increasing in number. The better papers will do the same. The day of the newspaper is yet to come. In twenty years we, as a people, will consume many times the daily print per capita we now take in. Books also will multiply. Novel-reading is in its very infancy. And so of other fields. Meanwhile the library, on the one side, joins forces with those who work in the field of school attendance, and helps to give the youngest product of the schools at least a glimpse of the pleasures and profits of good books. On the other side, it tries to make itself, as it were, the universal journal, the newspaper of all time, the handy book of reference for the worker and the laboratory of the scholar.

MAKING A LIBRARY KNOWN

Address Delivered before the Long Island Library Club, 1905

In making a library known the first and best of all its own agencies is, of course, the delivery desk. At this place more people learn what the library is, how it conducts itself, what it wishes to do and what it is doing in the community, than anywhere else. At this place, also, visitors to the library get their impression of the administration of the institution. Here they learn to like or dislike it, to approve or disapprove of it, to wish it well or to criticize it, to give it sympathy and aid, or neglect and discouragement.

It is a commonplace that the most efficient people in a library, those best able both to attract and to help others, should be detailed to meet the public at the delivery desk. Unfortunately, owing to the way in which libraries are now organized, it is difficult to place many of the best of the staff at this point. I grow each year stronger in the opinion that the purchase, reception, indexing and general preparation for the shelves of books have withdrawn from the work of getting in touch with the public too much of the library's originality and skill. The catalogue has become, in a measure, to libraries an old man of the sea. Let us treat our books more simply, and our readers more skilfully. After all, an index is but a tool.

It is the newspapers, of course, which of all outside agencies chiefly help to make the library known. I do not need to enlarge on their almost universal sympathy with the work of the library, their unfailing courtesy toward it, their readiness to print material in regard to it, even although it must often seem to the editors not to have a very strong newsy flavor. A librarian must, of course, bring the material he wishes printed to the attention of the newspapers in the right way. His library must in the first place have that attitude toward the public which the newspaper may readily expect the public to approve of. He makes it manifest, if he can, that he wishes to have the library's door sill worn down as fast as possible by the coming and going of the feet of those who built and maintain it.

Having made it plain that this is the general attitude of the library, he then presents the specific material he wishes to have printed in as attractive form as possible. The notes he sends, usually typewritten, are items of news, brief and plain, rather than demands or complaints. Most particularly he tries to keep the newspapers in touch with all changes and modifications of system. Nothing is better for a public institution than publicity. The people who pay for its support are entitled to know—it is a part of their education to know—all its ins and outs, its receipts, its expenditures, its methods, its plans and ambitions. Newspapers are almost invariably willing to insert these brief notes. They feel that about the management of a public library there should not be, toward the public, the slightest intimation of a desire for secrecy. I learned this lesson well from that best of American newspapers, the Springfield Republican. Of course there are matters of petty and personal detail and subjects under consideration to publish which would show poor judgment or poor taste. The newspapers understand this.

To illustrate what I have been saying about the courtesy of the newspapers toward libraries and their evident belief that libraries are engaged in educational work, and proper to be noted frequently in their columns, I have caused to be clipped from the newspapers in Newark all the things that have appeared about the library during thirty days. These items I have mounted on cardboard with notes to show when and where they appeared. They were published in three newspapers of Newark, two daily and one Sunday paper. They are thirty-one in number.

The longer articles, as you will see, are reports of, or papers read at, the meeting of the New Jersey Library Association at Asbury Park on October 18. I include them with the others because they went to the papers from the Newark Library, and were prepared at that library for the press. And furthermore, the Newark librarian was the president of the association at that meeting and thought it his duty to secure as far as possible the publication of its proceedings.

This showing of what the newspapers of a town have done for their public library in thirty days is more significant of the journals' good will toward the library than anything I can say.

The next in order is perhaps the catalogue, meaning by this printed book lists and bulletins, or whatever form it may take. The question of the advisability of having a complete catalogue of a library in one volume I cannot now go into. In a large town, where many cannot go to the library, a brief author list of all of the most important books in it seems to be quite an essential thing, though few libraries can now afford it. As to bulletins and lists in general, I am sure they should usually be made many, small and simple, instead of few, large and all-inclusive. The eight-page bulletin, for example, containing a list of all the books added to the library in a month, is almost as expensive as the same list printed on eight separate sheets. In the latter form it can be given entire to any borrower who wishes the whole list. One of the sheets meets the wishes of nearly all the persons who care to take a list away. Lists thus published give eight times as many lists for the same money.

These lists should be simple in their entries, without change in style and size of type, and without undue prominence given to the numbers. The more like ordinary reading matter the entry for the book is made, the more likely the ordinary reader is to understand it. These lists, especially if brief and devoted to some one topic, can be to good advantage mailed to persons in the town who are known to be interested in special subjects.

Work done for and through the schools comes next in order. Every teacher is a possible promoter of the library's work. She can win to it every year, if she will, forty or fifty friends in her pupils, and through them can win to its advocacy, and in a measure to its use, almost as many families. Small wonder that we ask the schools to help us! It is the library's place to be of use to them; it is the library's good fortune if it have the skill to win their good will and active aid.

If the library has a room in which meetings—educational, charitable and civic—can be held, these meetings may almost be placed next in order among the library's agencies for making itself known. Most libraries are far too conservative in this matter. Few will remain so long. The schools are beginning to show us the way. We are to have Sunday lectures in the Newark Library, the school authorities having led the way by granting for that purpose buildings which a short time ago were thought sacred to the children's weekday work.

MAKING A LIBRARY KNOWN

The work which the library does for and with the study clubs and volunteer organizations of all kinds in its town is, of course, one of the good ways of making itself known, felt and appreciated. If the clubs meet in the library building the work for them is by so much the easier and more effective as a means of publicity. Many organizations have received much assistance from libraries in the way of suggestions, books and pictures. I believe the time is coming when they will go a step further and ask the libraries to provide them with courses of study. This is more likely to happen if libraries can secure the cooperation of experts in colleges and other places in the compilation of such courses.

Circulars of all kinds and personal notes are helpful in bringing the library to the attention of individuals. Sometimes a weekly or monthly bulletin is sent to a group of people like the teachers or the members of some organization.

It is desirable to bring the library to the attention of busy professional men and students, even those who have collections of their own and rarely use the library. These can sometimes be reached by sending to them a few times in each winter a postal card telling them that a certain book has just been received at the library, and will be held for a time, in case they care to see it.

Posters and bulletins hung in conspicuous places throughout the city are useful methods of gaining the attention of many. Posters, like book lists and circulars, should be as brief as posssible. They should be well printed, and in case they are hung in hotel corridors, barber shops and other public places, they should be neatly and simply framed.

Exhibitions in the library, either of material belonging to the library itself or of paintings or other things lent for the purpose, in many cases draw many to the institution. These exhibitions, like some of the other things I have mentioned, are oftentimes more helpful in making the library known through the opportunity they give for newspaper note and comment, than through the actual visits paid to them by people interested. Whether or no much time should be spent in making a display or exhibition would seem to depend entirely on local conditions—the character of the library and of its community. The exact benefits that may be derived from this as from most other forms of advertising, it is impossible to estimate.

Delivery and deposit stations bring the library to the very doors of many people in the city who never can visit the main building itself. Delivery stations seem a particularly unsympathetic way of getting books into people's hands. The arm's length method of selecting through a catalogue, the many disappointments because of the constant demand for the new books, of which the supply is always inadequate, these alone discourage many from the continued use of the delivery station. The deposit station, a small collection of books placed in a store on open shelves and cared for by the storekeeper—this seems more successful. It is a representative of the library itself instead of the mere shadow thereof in the way of a book list.

Home libraries have been very useful where carefully and skilfully administered and have resulted in putting the library on a good footing with some of the people most difficult to reach. An objection to them is that if they are to be successful they must be carried on by skilled workers, workers who have been trained in the best methods of what is called settlement work, and such people are not often found on the staff of a public library.

Into the librarian's own personal work in a community it is, of course, impossible to go in detail. He or she belongs to certain clubs and organizations. He, perhaps, makes many helpful acquaintances through a church, perhaps, through organizations like social clubs, perhaps, through business associations like a board of trade. All of these forms of personal work will be found to draw attention in the right way to the library itself. The librarian must be well known if his library is, for he cannot, being a public servant, divorce himself in the public mind from the institution he administers.

Professional organizations like the national and state and local library associations give the librarian an opportunity—as you give me to-day—to present the work of his library to his constituents in a way which attracts their attention and informs them. Few citizens are slow to see that it is to their advantage to have their public servant, the librarian, interest himself in library meetings, make himself known as one proud of their library, interested in their industries and progress, glad of an opportunity to represent their city and wishing always to learn of his colleagues their latest and best ideas for adoption in his own community. I think it quite proper that I take advantage of the invitation you have kindly given me to speak to you to show you by indirection how proud Newark is of her beautiful library building and how generous she is in her wish that the institution which lives in it be active, helpful, and well advertised.

WHAT STATE AND LOCAL LIBRARY ASSOCIATIONS CAN DO FOR LIBRARY INTERESTS

Address Delivered before the American Library Association Conference, Portland, 1905

In one of the great books of the world, written about fifty years ago, the author has a chapter or two on man's mental and moral faculties. In them he tells how, as he modestly ventures to imagine it, men learned to bě moral, to have a feeling for conduct, to think of other men as possessed of rights, to be at peace with others, to understand others, to get help from others, to work with others for a common end, to cooperate. to organize. This process, all compact with thought and feeling, this growth of the animal into man, has been long continued; it still goes on; it may never end.

Now, it is far in thought from the snarling of the white and yellow dogs of war in eastern Asia to our gathering of peaceful bookmen for mutual aid and consolation. Yet the two events illustrate at once the conditions from which we have come and the progress we have made. It pays, we now say, for some to work together; and it pays, we still say, for some to fight one another. That is our conclusion; thus far, and thus far only, the race has gone in that slow march toward humanity which Darwin so simply outlined fifty years ago.

This is a large text for a humble theme. But why not begin with the obvious? If ever they seem of doubtful value—these organizers of ours—let us remind ourselves that by such in good part has man learned to be his neighbor's neighbor and that neighbor's fellow-citizen. To work with your fellows to a

123

common end—this is to be civilized, to be moral, to be efficient. This makes nations possible and promises the parliament of the world.

And so, in speaking of associations of librarians the first thing to be said is, that they effect so much by the mere fact that they are. They do so much of which we are but vaguely conscious, they so often give to so many without outward sign that subtle feeling of comradeship which becomes before one knows it a stimulus to further effort and a guide to that effort's profitable expense. One may well say, then, that the best work of an association is the association itself.

To put it more definitely, and to point to some of the secondary gains, we can say that to organize an association, no matter how poorly attended its meetings may be, teaches much to those who organize it, if to no others. You need not fear over-organization. Take your lesson from modern industrialism. Be sure that the laws of nature hold here as elsewhere and that the useless disappears. Seize the opportunity to get lessons in management and the art of working together. Moreover, the meeting which you carefully plan, provide speakers for, advertise among your colleagues, announce in the papers and duly hold, though attended by but the proverbial two or three, has served well; it has stimulated those who prepared for it, has made your calling more favorably known, and so has had its use. One may even say that, after all, it were often almost as well did the well-planned meeting never take place, so effective in education is its making, so meagre often are the tangible results on its appointed day.

My theme is mutual aid as a mark of progress, as an aid to progress, as civilization itself. The moral is, establish library associations. The special application is to the Pacific coast; and the illustrative examples are in the list which I offer you in printed form of the library associations and clubs of the world, 77 in number, 57 of them in the United States with a total of over 8,000 memberships. How inspiring is the story they tell of the growth of the library idea among us in the last thirty years.

In the West particularly you will find many intelligent readers, not at all connected with libraries, who are interested in library associations. Do not be discouraged by the small number in your own vicinity of those who are of your own calling. The tools of all the professional classes are books. Discussions on books, their making, their indexing in library catalogs, their selection, and their care, will always attract book-users. You have teachers' associations, and they are always ready to give up a part of their meetings to the discussion of library questions. A library department in a teachers' association can often do much to bring the library question into view.

And the vast distances which separate the western librarians must not discourage them. Their large meetings must be few, and even small ones may be difficult. Therefore more must be done at each possible library center. Let a few come together, organize in a simple way, call on all interested to support them, exploit their aims and methods freely in the newspapers, prepare a program of as general interest as possible, rather literary than technical, hold meetings, no matter how light the attendance, and publish through the papers a full report of proceedings.

I have said enough about the value of such work to those who carry it through; but too much cannot be said about the value to your calling of discreet and dignified publicity. We have not enough libraries yet, so we assume; and those we have, we frankly admit, fail by much of reaching their highest efficiency. We wish to impress our fellows with a sense of the value of libraries to their communities. Then, we wish to show how easy it is for any community to establish and support it. Then, we wish to learn from one another and to call forth from the public criticisms and suggestions. The newspapers like to help us to do these things. They can be done, with their help, by one person. They can be better done, usually, by three or four. They can be done better still, usually, by an organization with a name, an object, officers, meetings, and reports. This is sound psychological theory. It has worked well many times in practice.

Let me be still more specific, for I am warned that my talk must be practical.

You are, we will suppose, the one person in your community who is interested in public libraries; you may be a librarian and wish to join with the two or three other library workers in your part of the state in learning more of your calling and in increasing library interest; or you may have no library in your place and wish to see one established. You send to your library commission or to the A. L. A. headquarters, or to any librarian of experience and ask for suggestions. These being considered you look at your own problem, select the people likely to help you, two or three, and talk the subject over with each of them. Then you lay your plans and form a rather definite scheme. You ask your friends to come together and you put your ideas before them; and, as you know your ground and know what you want, you push them through. The meeting votes for an organization; appoints one or two to bring in a constitution and a list of officers; and, if it seem wise, you complete the organization at one sitting. You need not have money to print constitutions and by-laws and officers, for the newspapers will do it for you.

Next comes a meeting. You study first the audience you may get—the minister, the teacher, the reading women, and other possibles—and decide what topics will most interest them. Perhaps such as these: "Our present library laws and how they apply in our town." "How they started the library in Blankville"—another small town in your state. "How libraries are helping the school teachers"; and, for the general reader, "The three best novels of the year." The meeting place is a private house, or the school-house, or a church. See to it yourself that the newspaper tells about all these things.

The smaller your town the larger the audience, relatively, that you will get. You have prepared for absences of speakers, you have arranged for some to speak on call on the subject that you select, you leave nothing to spontaneous, unconsidered utterance; for though you hope there may be free discussion you do not depend on it for any points you wish to make. You prepare the report for the paper yourself. If the nearest available one is small and can only print a brief report, you abstract the speeches, enlarge on the purpose of the movement, and name the names of those most interested.

I dwell on the obvious; but with good reason. My list shows that there are many library associations, yet observation has taught us that few of them are ever properly effective. The one moving, pushing, persistent person is lacking; too much dependence is put on the meeting itself; not enough is won from preparation for it or from the proper publicity it can induce. And so I think it no fault that I urge again that you yourself be the one efficient person, and that you remember always that it is the organization's daily life throughout the year and the story thereof which chiefly help your calling. The meetings may be much, the constant strivings between them may be much more. It is not simply for these A. L. A. gatherings we have so much enjoyed that some have crossed a continent. You of the West and we of the East—and the you and we include those at home as well as those here—have for these ten months been looking forward to this gathering, have had our thoughts turned often to our great northwest and to the nourishing of libraries therein, and have gained thereby a broader view. I am sure I speak for my eastern colleagues as well as for myself when I say that to contemplate our western empire and to consider the task awaiting our Pacific friends and the brave beginnings they have made induce a most excellent state of sanctified humility. Praise be to the A. L. A. which brings us here, and to our western friends who persuaded us to come!

I have touched on the details of the smallest library association. Let me say something also of the larger ones, usually easy to form, often given to sounding brass and tinkling cymbals, sometimes dying and quite unmindful of the fact, and never as effective as opportunity permits.

They are often too conservative. They think it is their wisdom which restrains them, while in fact it is simply their mediocrity. They rise no higher than their average. They repress the aggressive and the original. They fear they may do something improper, and, clothed in perfect propriety, they reach long before they are aware of it a Nirvana of noble inutility. For special sins, common, but of course not universal, they make their meetings too long. In their zeal to make many good points they fail of one. They crowd their programs until they are dizzily and tediously encyclopedic. They fail in hospitality, and the members gather solemnly and glare at one another across a crowded room and pass out again with never a gain in fellowship. They harp too much on one string; or they talk unconsidered prattle about details which only carefully chosen words can set duly forth. They parade their fluent speakers until their meetings become little more than one voice crying in a wilderness of inattentive ears. They do not give the timid a chance, rather they don't compel the shy to take up their burdens and talk. They bring the heads, the chiefs, forever into gatherings with the assistants and check that outpouring of the spirit which the latter would delight in. They do not cultivate the art of provoking and guiding discussion. They look for a crop of spontaneous ideas in a soil which does not grow them. They do not make sure that from the floor, at the call of the chairman, shall come, in seeming impromptu, the best things of the day. They do not work together as they should. Every club and association in the country, more than fifty of them, should be in touch with the A. L. A., and so with each other. Every member of each and every association should be made to feel that by joining her own association she becomes united with the national organization and will get something from it. They do not

—the larger and stronger clubs are the more able in this direction and thereby the greater sinners— make themselves of direct use to the community of readers at large by producing work of practical value to readers and students. The hundreds of libraries and library workers, gathered within some of the great eastern cities, have, in the ecstasy of self-contemplation, quite forgotten to gather the golden fruit of opportunity—and I speak as one of the sinners.

Further, these larger organizations, and the smaller, too, are not sufficiently careful about the place of meeting, that it be dignified, homelike, and quiet. For any save very large meetings, they forget that a platform and footlights or anything approaching them are fatal.

Once more, associations large and small and especially the larger ones, usually fail not only to carry through each year some work of permanent value to the profession and to general and special students—work like annotated book lists, study courses, brief manuals on the use of books, general or special—they fail also sufficiently to acquaint the public through the press with the possible utilities of a public library. By nature the bookman is a gentle and retiring creature. He likes his library and takes proper pride in it. He helps to organize a club, by joining it at least, and then contents himself with the glow of comradeship which comes therefrom. The possible public influence of the instrument he has helped to fashion is not well discerned. Every club should provide for the publication, from week to week or from month to month, of notes on the elements of librariology. Librariology is the knowledge of libraries and the art of using them. No important journal in the country is more ready to aid the library movement or more able to do it intelligently than the New York Independent. A recent editorial in its columns on "Libraries for men" shows how far we have come from making clear to editors what a library is, to say nothing of what it hopes and tries to be. If the Independent is still thus untaught, how unskilled in librariology must be the average of men. You in the West will repair this lack, I am sure, sooner than we of the East. Precedents and conventions rule you less. You will individually when you can, and through your clubs always, keep up a stream of expository contributions on librariology in your daily and weekly press. The East is coming to realize the need of these forms of activity. The A. L. A. has now both the disposition and the means, not only to do good things for readers, but also to inform the public of the existence, the character and the possibilities for usefulness of collections of books. Shall I be more specific? Need I refer again to the committee on publicity long ago advocated and never yet realized? Can I say, without being misunderstood, that to publish an "A. L. A. catalog" and an A. L. A. Booklist is not enough? That if a health food is worth wide advertising, surely these library products also are? That 160 library people should spend nearly $40,000 to cross the continent and meet with you, was not this such an indication of library progress as the public generally would like to hear of?

After I have had my first say I am ready always to give ear to But and If and Remember and Perhaps. You may attach them to these suggestions as you will. I will myself add but one. It is this: Remember, that after all if you wish a certain specific thing done, you must do it yourself. The crowd has the passing emotion, the one man brings tireless zeal. Don't think an organization is an end. If a good club is the work of your hands, do not think it useful unless it does something. We can't conquer the public with our clubs. Moreover, never let your association hamper its strongest members. Democracy is the apotheosis of mediocrity. If the many would advance they must look to the leader to guide them. In union is strength; but the worth of strength is in its use. An association tends to the academic and to hold its members to a standard, often a narrow one.

I return once more to my text, mutual aid, as at once progress itself and the measure of civilization, and to one of its general applications, an appeal for practice in the art of organizing. If we join with our fellows for an end of value to us all, we learn thus far to love our neighbor in the best possible and the only universally acceptable way—through finding him useful and ourselves inspired.

In Newark we have made a rough check-list of all the voluntary organizations of the city, religious, educational, industrial, philanthropic, beneficiary. In a population of 270,000, largely foreign, we find 2,700 of these with about 25,000 officials, and with a total estimated membership of 190,000. We hope to make use of more of these organizations than we have heretofore by appealing to more of them through the books which touch on the subjects for which, directly or indirectly, they are organized. I mention them here only to emphasize my statement that we have learned that it pays sometimes to work with our neighbors and not always to fight them; and to illustrate the old doctrine, now sometimes forgotten, that those who work together of their own free will thereby build a better civilization, on the firm basis of profitable fellowship, than was ever built on laws, whether enforced by emperors or democracies. The conclusion is, encourage your colleagues, confer with them, work with them, and as opportunity permits join with them in organized effort to attain certain definite results. So doing you get wisdom for yourself and growth in esteem and efficiency for your profession.

MANY-SIDED INTEREST: HOW THE LIBRARY PROMOTES IT

School Journal, December 22, 1906

I believe that libraries are for scholars; that they should supply the material which studious and thoughtful men need in pursuing their studies and ripening their thoughts. In libraries the lamp of learning should be kept always lighted, that here men of study and reflection—the guides we must always come to at the last—may relight if need be their several torches. I believe that libraries are for delights, and should contribute directly to the happiness of their people. I believe that libraries are for other purposes also. I wish now to set forth my belief that libraries should serve as incentives and stimulants; that they should try by all proper methods to increase the interest their constituents take in the world they live in, to the end that those constituents, the people, may find that the library they have set up has helped them to become broader, more generous-minded, better balanced and more able and willing to work for the common welfare with their neighbors—with their neighbors who are both their fellow-countrymen and their fellows of other countries. The library should be a mental irritant in the community; it should help to make the old fresh, the strange tolerable, the new questionable, and all things wonderful. I believe this because I think most people are too well satisfied with their own narrow lives, and do not take interest enough in the life about them; if they took more interest in it they would understand each other better, would work together better, and would make this a more peaceful, more effective and happier world.

Let me restate this ancient creed in another way. A secret of happiness is accomplishment. This is as true of a people as of a person. A people's power of accomplishment is their social efficiency.

The secret of social efficiency is voluntary organization: not governmental organization, which is compulsory, but the free organization to which we chiefly owe our industrial development, our esthetic, our social, and our religious life.

This voluntary organization is voluntary cooperation—to restate it in terms which make prominent its essential points of skill, free choice, and mutual aid.

The secret of cooperation is enlightened sympathy. Not pity, not condescension, but kinship of thought through feeling, through the good will which accompanies a clear understanding of the views of life, the prejudices, the creeds, and the aims of others.

The secret of sympathy is likeness in custom, ideal, and aim. How and why sympathy springs from similarity in manners, morals, and purpose is still a secret; but we know that we work gladly and well with those whose manners, though they differ from our own, we are wonted to; whose ideals, though they differ from our own, we know are not bad; whose ambitions, though not ours, we find lead to no harm.

The public library, like the public school is the product of mutual aid, of a cooperation primarily voluntary. It is in turn itself a factor, and as such adds to social efficiency not by teaching directly how effectively to organize and cooperate, but by promoting sympathy. It exposes to many the similarities between manners, ideals, and aims which seem at first quite dissimilar. Government, diplomacy, war— these are on the surface in our relations with other nations, for example, the Orientals. These superficial international relations point to a substratum of individual ignorance, narrowness, and selfishness. We first ignore, then despise, then fear, then hate the alien. But contact opens our eyes. We soon find that though his manners are strange they are harmless; that though his ideals are curiously expressed, they are high; that though his aims are not what we inherit, they are worthy. Then we applaud, we sympathize, we cooperate—and peace is here.

The native antagonism of races is as I have said, an exaggerated form of the personal antagonism which is at large among us, and among all other peoples, and always will be, until knowledge begets sympathy and diversity of forms in manners, ideals, and aims is no longer taken for diversity in substance.

The library, in its efforts to expose to its constituents the likeness of their aims, customs, and morals, finds that as the secret of ignorance is indifference, so the secret of knowledge is interest. This secret is more important to library than to school. The school can compel to knowledge; the library must allure to knowledge. The schools are for educible young; the libraries are for persuadable old. The child is in the age of observation, acquisition, and change; the old are in the age of knowledge, conviction, and creed.

How then—and this is the library's question which is always waiting for more fullness of answer —how can the library arouse in its people an interest in the wide world? How can it prove itself the proper inheritor of the efficiency of the Athenian Gadfly? How make its supporters feel that this world is full of the permanent possibilities of pleasure? How make them realize that though wisdom linger when knowledge comes, without knowledge wisdom will not stir abroad? How show them that to be interested is to be laying up knowledge? that to have a many-sided interest is to have sympathy and willingness to cooperate? and that skill will follow? and that he who has power and will to cooperate has acquired a social education?

The good book is alive. A gathering of good books is an organization of the wise. Any library may stand idle, but every library has infinite capacity for good work. The library can hold its books to the simple task of giving strength, incentive, and guidance to the few who spontaneously seek them; just as the school can wait upon the call of the student who comes and asks its aid. But the library may also awaken interest and stimulate inquiry; just as the school summons the indifferent to its tasks by making plain the pleasures and profits of the knowledge it can give. But the school can also command attendance and compel study; while the library can invite and attract, but no more.

It is in the wide range of its powers, the variety of its profferings, and the number of its constituents that the library finds its advantages over school and college; and these same advantages assure the success of its efforts to add to the interest of life.

But first it must make known its powers. It is under the burden of misapprehension. Books were formerly for the bookish only. The bookish formed a class apart. They were literary in the old sense of the word. From those days comes the feeling that a public collection of books is a collection of literary books useful chiefly to the professed student of books and to the reader of *belles-lettres*. In my town a library can openly follow its mission for seventeen full years, and an active man of affairs in the town can still express surprise when he learns that his library will gladly answer his inquiries, to the full of its abilities, about the price of books, the choice of books, or the tests of wood-block paving. The instance is typical. The fact is told a thousand times yet it is still known to but few, that while the library is for students and readers it is not for them only, but is also for the daily use of every citizen. Just what this will mean in the life of our towns and cities, when all are awake to its possibilities, it is impossible to say. I am sure the librarian will then look on its figures of books lent as even less important than he considers them today.

First, then, I repeat, the library must make itself known, and it must make itself known, not so much as a library in the conventional sense of the word, as an index, easy to reach and easy to use, of all the facts of life, all the best theories of life, and all the skilfully woven fancies of life.

The newspapers, many of them at least, understand the library better than the librarian. They note that to its shelves come reports of all that the world is doing, saying, and dreaming, and they may well wonder that so little comes from them. The news is a little belated for morning scareheads, it is true; but in fullness, accuracy, and depth it excels. The librarian cannot retail this world-news through the daily press; but he can bring it nearer to his people than do a few figures of circulation and a bibliography of earthworms. The daily record of the library's additions to the possibilities of profit, pleasure, and wisdom on its shelves should fill a corner of the paper and be found of interest by

many. Librarians will know that I am not speaking
from experience. Rather, I am prophesying.

The library should be a commonplace to every one.
To use it should be as natural when one needs news
or knowledge, fiction or fact, as it is to use the trolley
when one needs transportation.

The telephone is the mutual friend of all. It is a
great leveler, and it adds a million strong-threads to
that great social fabric which we are all trying to
weave. It brings the library, in a sense, to every
fireside. That its use between the people and their
books has been so little is another indication of the
academic remoteness of the library. Having found
by telephone that the book, pamphlet, journal, catalog, quotation or what not is in the library, the
inquirer should be able to have it quickly brought to
him. Private enterprise delivers its goods; a public
institution can well imitate this example as far as
means permit.

The newspaper and the telephone bring the library
into the every-day world. The newspaper—I am
repeating my prophecy—shows from day to day how
the library gathers the best that is done and thought
and said in the world in every field. The morning
paper says that Peary failed; the library soon will
have in its books the story of the successes of his
failure. Santos-Dumont flies; Herculaneum is to be
excavated; the English soap trust dissolves; Japan
floats a ship of war;—these are the morning's notes.
Later the library offers the same, in book or journal,
carefully considered and set in proper relations. Of
each of these and ten thousand other things a few
wish to know the full truth. So far as the library
gets full and careful chronicles it should let their
coming be known. To do this requires scholarship,

of which our libraries have not enough. But parenthetically let me say that they never did have enough. Many of the old librarians were readers, few of them were students. They cultivated the muses; but the muses did not respond. Their admirers mistook a cheerful literary geniality for high converse and apt reference to the learned for learning itself.

Often it is possible for the library, by note, or postal, or brief list, to send to the one or the few in its city that word about book or journal which is just what he needs. In time the organized special information work of a public library will be very great. Many will ask for what they need when they need it. Many will ask, also, to be told when that which they need comes to the library shelf. Private enterprises can clip you the notes you wish from a thousand journals as they appear. Surely a public institution, for a moderate fee, if need be, can furnish notes of books and articles on special subjects.

If you say all this is informing the library's constituents and not interesting them, then I have not made my chief point plain. The library contains information, more or less full and recent according to its resources, on every subject that every person in its city finds it interesting and profitable to know about. And if there is any subject which would interest any of its people did they chance to hear of it—about that subject also the library has information. Now, given a storehouse like this, if it make itself widely known for what it is, present interests will be fed, new interests will be aroused.

I am aware that these remarks smell more of commerce than of the lamp. The old-fashioned student, if he heard them, might well ask where he can find, under the conditions I suggest, that old-fashioned library with its penetralia perfumed with emanations from ancient volumes in which the old-fashioned librarian pores over books that are books and joins with inquiring spirits in peaceful dialog. Let me say to this that I began with the axiom that libraries are for scholars. Then let me add that every library, even though the rumor get abroad that the active motion within it has penetrated the places some would wish reserved for the spirits of the dead and the meditations of quietists—every libra , I say, no matter how grievously awake and sinfully modern it may be, can furnish a quiet corner for rumination. Every librarian delights in its readers. If to any the old books and a place apart are of the essence of library enjoyment, these the librarian can provide and will with pleasure.

Then let me add that the disturbance of that fine quietude which old folios, disintegrating leathers, ancient dust, and venerable readers typify, by change, newness and restless use, is not a new thing. Had Cæsar perfected for Rome the great public library he planned it would not have been an abode simply for the ancient browsers of the day—unless we are quite mistaken in our Cæsar. When all the libraries of Rome rejected Ovid's books as not fit for their readers, the wits surely had their joke about silly and presumptious censors of morals and the passing of the good old times when libraries let the wise choose their own reading. The latter-day librarian, one says, is too commercial and talks too much of methods of persuasion and conducts his place as if readers were not born, but made by advertising. Well, the Ptolemies ransacked the world for books and then that these might not uselessly lie idle provided food and lodgings for the readers they invited! To this, with all its modernity, the American free public library has not yet come. Lipsius asked, three centuries ago, why gather books if they are not to be freely used? Mazarin, fifty years later, was proud to open his library to all the world without excepting a living soul. These, mind you, are ancient ideas, not new ones. And it is cheering to feel that the librarian of to-day is awakening at last to their full import.

The library, then, should be accumulative of books; hospitable to students; a sedative for quietists, and provocative of interests—and the last is not least. To be stimulating it must be known, easily reached, and by post and telephone easily bespoken.

The rest of my argument is not so easily set down. I wish to touch in a few words on some of the activities which, in harmony with the thought that a people's books should broaden and multiply that people's interest, emanate from or find their first movements within our modern libraries. Again I do not speak from experience or from the history of any one library. I say simply that things like these are done in this, that, and the other village, town, or city; not all in any one.

A lecturer of note is coming; a famous opera is revived; the art of printing is discussed; the river front is to be redeemed; the smoke nuisance is to be abated; the library sets forth in newspaper or special list the best and latest writings on each and every one of these topics.

The town needs a museum of art, of science, of local history; the library is among the first to note the fact; by letters, lectures, and references to appropriate books and pamphlets it brings the need home to the few best fitted to consider their advantages and opens a corner in the library to the humble beginnings of one or all of them.

Foreigners, knowing no English, flock to the factories. The library calls in the children, and gives them the English books they ask for; through them it attracts the parents; learns that the latter wish to read of their new country in their own tongue; finds that there are no books in foreign languages which simply and briefly describe us and our ways, and sets to work to have them written.

Posters about the library go up in railway stations, trolley cars, and other public places.

Lecture courses are given in library halls and at them the library's appropriate books and lists thereof are shown and distributed.

Children whose homes are without books, ideas, or reading habits are taught the pleasures of literature by wise story-tellers and skilful readers.

Branches are set up here and there in cities; books are sent by the basketful from the village library to country cross roads; open cases full of books are put in stores; tiny libraries are sent to homes in remote corners of the city and to lone farmhouses among the hills; a library agent tours a state, enlightens, interests, instructs, and exhorts by turns in every village and town—all to the end that more may find pleasure and profit from books and through them multiply their interests, moderate their prejudices, and broaden their sympathies.

In due course every school-room becomes a library, every teacher a librarian, and every pupil is encouraged to form the habit of reading good things and collecting ideas.

The library displays collections of beautiful

things. The sciences and the trades also are shown, and the library becomes now a miniature museum of some industry, now of some art.

The story could go on through many other details; and you may think it strange that one ventures to say it is not enough. In answer let me say that, for all our eighty million, we publish few of the best books, we do not maintain properly a single weekly or monthly journal of high scholarship, we are self-centered, unduly prejudiced in our judgments, and are thoughtless and clamant hero-worshippers. Our published utterances are what we should expect. Out of the conflict between them come many sparks of wit, but these rarely flame up into the clear light of sound learning. We need to feel that others also think, and think with care and with background of more learning than is given to many of our people to acquire. In the libraries are the books of the wise; the very souls of the wise. We are all learning to read; perhaps the library will in time learn how to induce more to read the best. If many read the best, interests will multiply and deepen and, if Herbart was not mistaken, broader views will be taken and wiser councils will more often prevail.

Our Lindsay Swift laments the day "when the cry went forth that the librarian must be a business man and not a scholar." The edge of his kindly wit is turned a bit when we recall that he is himself in the library business; and we feel that so long as libraries find his like useful, scholarship is not forbidden among us! Also we may take his humor with better grace, if we remember that while many may refine subtly on the violin, flute, and other tender instruments, for a complete orchestra one at least must beat the drum. And, once more, it had been a sad day indeed if the cry had gone forth "that the librarian must be a scholar and not a business man."

Through all this paper I have assumed, what librarians know quite well, that in a library's books are found all the interests of life; I point my story once more by saying that it is one of the library's duties to make known to its people that this is true; and that in their books are all the thoughts and deeds and dreams of all men, and that through these their books they may get the broad and wholesome view of things.

If I speak too much of the art of making things known to others, of helping others to find that this is an entrancing world of wonderful deeds and charming fancies and humorous contrasts, and if I say too little about our own shortcomings, I do not regret it, for I confess I am just now beating the drum. A sentence of Pater's, which I paraphrase, may help you to see my point of view. "To his pious recognition of that one orderly spirit—scholarship—which diffuses itself through the world and animates it, the librarian adds a warm personal devotion towards the whole multitude of the old gods—the good books—and one new one besides—utility—by him we hope not ignobly conceived."

ANTICIPATIONS, OR WHAT WE MAY EXPECT IN LIBRARIES[1]

Public Libraries, December, 1907

The newspapers will more and more usurp the work of libraries. They will be printed in larger type and on better paper. They will be systematically arranged, and will have digests and indexes. In their magazine departments they will publish novels, essays, poems, dramas, histories and biographies by the best writers of the day, as well as the results of the cogitations of the best philosophers, the anticipations of the best sociologists and the conclusions of the best scientists. Their illustrations will be superior to the finest that books now offer. The Sunday supplements whose pictures are to-day so scorned and condemned by those who wish to be thought extra dainty and refined, but are really dull and unimaginative—these Sunday supplements suggest what newspapers will soon furnish us in art and illustrations. Truly, the newspapers will be our educational salvation, for they will enable us to acquire in the simplest and quickest way, by pictures, at least a little of the vast mass of information which the world's web of wires, reticulation of rails and fleets of ocean ferries will daily bring to us.

We are just learning to read newspapers. When all of us—not a few only, but all of us—truly have the newspaper habit, the demand will bring forth sheets such as now are not dreamed of. Yellows to the yellow minded—and both will be with us for many a day. But the mechanism and brains and skill are here to produce, and the sufficient demand

[1] Read before the N. J. Library Association, Trenton.

which is sure to come may any day call forth, a daily paper of clearness, accuracy, breadth, simplicity and beauty far beyond the wildest prophecies of the most optimistic editor.

The future of the library, then, seems on first thought to be simple desuetude. But not altogether. The library will still be useful as storehouse, index and guide. It will gather and preserve the best of the world's books; these it will by more simple and so more useful catalogs make more readily accessible to students; and its curators will become wiser guides to the whole realm of knowledge.

Books will be more freely discarded than at present, leaving us thus a more easily handled residuum of useful material. In a few places there will be great storehouses where moribund books will repose by the millions. The ephemeral character of nearly all print will be freely admitted; and books will have value in almost all libraries because they are of use, not because some casual historical or anecdotal prowler happens to wish to use them. That is, it will soon not be held that a book is useful, simply because once last year a man chanced to ask for it.

The catalog on cards may stay; but the catalog in print will surely return. It is easy now to imagine a modified linotype machine, casting title-a-line book lists, in a large-faced type, on long light slugs only one-eighth the present needless height. These will be as easily handled and arranged as cards, can be so made as to be set in columns, locked into forms of newspaper size and stereotyped readily—and there you are, with a catalog printed like the New York Herald, in one page or a hundred; easily consulted, cheap, and as it should be, ephemeral; ephemeral, of course, for in the anticipated library the changes by discards and additions will make any catalogue out of date in ten days.

The charging system will grow simpler. In the small library any method will serve; in the larger one time and trouble must be saved. The borrower's card is a burden. Perhaps a numbered metal slip will serve in its place; a slip which the elect can secure in gold and wear as a watch charm. But surely the future library will dispense with the card for the borrower. Every city has a directory, why not use it? Would not a number beside the name of each borrower nearly fill the needs of the delivery desk, with a short list arranged by numbers written in another book.

This is not the time for details, for we must pass on to the aeroplanes which will leave the delivery station on the roof every fifteen minutes and, dividing the city into precincts, will call daily at the library windows of every house in town. Here we see librarians assaulting high heavens in balloons, having purged the lower world of slums with Home Libraries and Story Tellers. These aeroplanes will supplant the house-to-house delivery of books, long an accomplished fact; but will not entirely do away with the magnificent automobile and trolley-car libraries, commodious, attractive, carrying several thousand influential books and a persuasive librarian, now gliding swiftly through the city, now pausing at a street corner long enough to exude a few books.

Also here is the automatic delivery room. This is the thing you are looking for. The latest books, a thousand titles more or less, stand in cases that look like automatic venders of tutti-frutti chewing gum, except for pictures of Minerva on their fronts and busts of Marion Crawford on their tops. In these,

149

marvellously like cuds of gum in their shape and in the cozy way they lie together, are the books that most desire. Each borrower has a tiny strip of metal, not larger than a Yale lock key. This he drops into the proper place in the stand which holds the books he wishes, presses a button, and, behold! his book!—or, a nicely printed card saying, "not in at present." An ingenious mechanism, actuated by the notches on the borrower's check, has meanwhile charged the book to his number. A kindred labor-saving device credits him with a book returned when he inserts his check in the proper place to open the slot through which he passes the book he brought back. When restaurants have automatic waiters it is time for libraries to use automatic delivery rooms.

Librarians and assistants will, in the future, take time to read a little; but this is less an anticipation than an aspiration.

Inquirers will not expect libraries to fit them out with thoughts any quicker than a ready-made clothing store can fit them out with clothes. Questions of importance will be answered by persons equal to the task. But many hundred carefully selected inquiries, made repeatedly at all libraries and evidently passed on by inheritance from parent to children, always heretofore fully and courteously answered by attendants, will be replied to by the "automatic Who, What, and Why Machine." On the front of an attractive case are several hundred push buttons; below each button is a little label, bearing a question; all the questions are arranged under subjects and then sub-divided under the words, Who, What, Which, Why, etc. The inquirer finds the question he wishes to ask, pushes the proper button, and at once a card rises above the case bearing the complete and accurate answer. Many will come to scoff at this machine; all will stay to use it.

Another more elaborate machine answers more difficult, delicate and even quite personal questions; but is actuated only when a penny is dropped in a slot before a button is pushed. This is the famous Pay-Collection of Complete Answers of which you will soon have heard.

If stories are told to children they will be told by a phonograph, and the phonograph will be a block away from the library. For while the newspapers will take much of our work away, enough will remain within a very manifestly bookish field to leave no time to take up the tasks of the family fireside or the kindergarten. Moreover, we can easily make too much of the dear old stories. Like our patriotism, our religion, our ideals, our friendships and our loves, they are not for analyzing and flaunting, but for quiet absorption. Moreover, again, we are already too much subject to the hypnotic influence of the oratorical voice. Let the children practice asking questions instead of listening so much to stories of an age when kindness in the strong was thought a marvel; they may then acquire the habit; and when grown will ask more questions of their would-be oratorical bamboozlers, instead of applauding them. It is listening that has done the world so much harm, not talking.

The newspaper having largely supplanted the library, naturally there will be no occasion for the library to furnish newspapers. Reading rooms will disappear; study-rooms will take their places. These will be busy places with none of that somniferous Air of the Rest-cure Establishment nowadays much complained of. The Fairy Prince of Thoughtfulness will here be continually awakening the Sleeping

LIBRARIES

Beauties of Indolence. Mind will conquer Matter,
and though many may still dream in the public library
none will resort to it to knit up the ravell'd sleave of
care.

But, if you listen attentively, you will hear a
cheerful, well modulated voice calling out the titles of
books and dilating briefly on their contents. It ap-
proaches the end of the alphabet. "Weariness in
Audiences," it says, "six by nine inches, 127 pages,
10-point Scotch Roman type, well printed, neatly
bound; pictures of audiences at ease, in commotion,
asleep, awake, and very tired. Popular with political orators; useful to association 'Jiners.' Full
directions on 'How to stop when you have talked
enough.' Examples from ancient history. Special
references to J. C. Dana, one time of New Jersey.
Price $.50, very net."

That is a library megaphone calling out to-morrow's additions to the Trenton Public Library.

STORY-TELLING IN LIBRARIES

Public Libraries, November, 1908

Story-telling to groups of young children is now popular among librarians. The art is practiced chiefly by women. No doubt one reason for its popularity is that it gives those who practice it the pleasures of the teacher, the orator and the exhorter. It must be a delight to have the opportunity to hold the attention of a group of children; to see their eyes sparkle as the story unwinds itself; to feel that you are giving the little people high pleasure, and at the same time are improving their language, their morals, their dramatic sense, their power of attention and their knowledge of the world's literary masterpieces. Also, it is pleasant to realize that you are keeping them off the streets; are encouraging them to read good books; are storing their minds with charming pictures of life and are making friends for your library.

In explaining its popularity I have stated briefly the arguments usually given in favor of library story-telling. There is another side.

A library's funds are never sufficient for all the work that lies before it. Consequently, the work a library elects to do is done at the cost of certain other work it might have done. The library always puts its funds, skill and energy upon those things which it thinks are most important, that is, are most effective in the long run, in educating the community. Now, the schools tell stories to children, and it is obviously one of their proper functions so to do at such times, to such an extent and to such children as the persons in charge of the schools think wise.

It is probable that the schoolmen know better when and how to include story-telling in their work with a given group of children than do the librarians. If a library thinks it knows about this subject more than do the schools, should it spend time and money much needed for other things in trying to take up and carry on the schools' work? It would seem not. Indeed, the occasional story-telling which the one library of a town or city can furnish is so slight a factor in the educational work of that town or city as to make the library's pride over its work seem very ludicrous.

If, now, the library by chance has on its staff a few altruistic, emotional, dramatic and irrepressible child-lovers who do not find ordinary library work gives sufficient opportunities for altruistic indulgence, and if the library can spare them from other work, let it set them at teaching the teachers the art of story-telling.

Contrast, as to cost and results, the usual story-telling to children with instruction in the same and allied arts to teachers. The assistant entertains once or twice each week a group of forty or fifty children. The children—accustomed to schoolroom routine, hypnotized somewhat by the mob-spirit and a little by the place and occasion, ready to imitate on every opportunity—listen with fair attention. They are perhaps pleased with the subject matter of the tale, possibly by its wording, and very probably by the voice and presence of the narrator. They hear an old story, one of the many that help to form the social cement of the nation in which they live. This is of some slight value, though the story is only one of scores which they hear or read in their early years at school. The story has no special dramatic power in its sequence. As a story it is of value almost solely because it is old. It has no special value in its phrasing. It may have been put into artistic form by some man of letters; but the children get it, not in that form, but as retold by an inspired library assistant who has made no mark in the world of letters by her manner of expression. The story has no moral save as it is dragged in by main strength; usually, in fact, and especially in the case of myths, the moral tone needs apologies much more than it needs praise.

To prepare for this half hour of the relatively trivial instruction of a few children in the higher life, the library must secure a room and pay for its care, a room which if it be obtained and used at all could be used for more profitable purposes; and the performer must study her art and must, if she is not a conceited duffer, prepare herself for her part for the day at a very considerable cost of time and energy.

Now, if the teachers do not know the value of story-telling at proper times and to children of proper years; if they do not realize the strength of the influences for good that lies in the speaking voice—though that this influence is relatively over-rated in these days I am at a proper time prepared to show—if they do not know about the interest children take in legends, myths and fairy tales, and their value in strengthening the social bond, then let the library assistants who do know about such things hasten to tell them. I am assuming for purposes of argument that the teachers do not know, and that library assistants can tell them. I shall not attempt to say how the library people will approach the teacher with their information without offending them, except to remark that tactful lines of approach can be found;

and to remark, further, that by setting up a story-hour in her library a librarian does not very tactfully convey to the teachers the intimation that they either do not know their work or willfully neglect it.

With this same labor of preparation, in the room used for a thirty-minute talk to a handful of children, the librarian could far better address a group of teachers on the use of books in libraries and school-rooms. Librarians have long contended that teachers are deficient in bookishness; and it is quite possible that they are. Their preparation in normal schools compels them to give more attention to method than to subject matter. They have lacked incentive and opportunity to become familiar with books, outside of the prescribed text-books and supplementary readers. They do not know the literature of and for childhood, and not having learned to use books in general for delight and utility themselves they cannot impart the art to their pupils. As I have said, librarians contend that this is true, yet many of them with opportunities to instruct teachers in these matters lying unused before them, neglect them and coolly step in to usurp one of the school's functions and rebuke the teacher's shortcomings.

This is not all. A library gives of its time, money and energy to instruct forty children—and there it ends. If, on the other hand, it instructs forty teachers, those forty carry the instruction to forty class rooms and impart knowledge of the library, of the use of books, of the literature for children and—if need be—of the art of story-telling, to 1,600 or 2,000 children. There seems no question here as to which of these two forms of educational activity is for librarians better worth while.

WHAT THE MODERN LIBRARY IS DOING.

Independent, January 26, 1911

Modern library methods began with the meeting of a few librarians at the Centennial Exhibition in Philadelphia in 1876. These librarians formed an association and began the publication of a professional journal. Since that time the development of libraries, both public and collegiate, has in this country been perhaps more rapid than the development of any other public educational institution. The benefactions of philanthropists have had something to do with this rapidity of development. But before the habit of giving libraries had been taken up by the very rich, the movement toward the establishment and improvement of these institutions in our villages, towns and cities was well under way.

When librarians began to take an active interest in the improvement of their calling thirty years ago, they naturally first turned their attention to the technique of administration. This was the era of book-shelf, book-storage, catalog, classification, accession book, shelf-list, and of all the many other improvements in keeping, handling and indexing books.

Then came the era of library buildings, partly due, as suggested already, to the benefactions of the unduly rich; an era of the development of some baneful tendencies, from which libraries have not yet recovered, and will not for many years. Trustees of town and city libraries and trustees of colleges and universities were for a time overcome, and many of them are still overcome, with the desire to erect monuments of their own day of brief authority, and architects were ready to take advantage of human weakness in this direction. Nine out of ten of the college and town and city library buildings in this country, built within the past twenty years, are too small, or improperly arranged, or hideously ugly, or all three; and this although in almost every case a proper building could have been erected for the money lavished on an inadequate structure, or a very monstrosity.

Next came an era of publicity. The movement in this direction has not yet been carried as far as it might well be. In a few communities it is now well understood that a proper part of the library's work is to make itself fully known to its constituents and possible users; but it is not yet realized by either public or college libraries that the public's expensive organizations which collect, store and lend books should also give unprejudiced information about them, and this as freely as publisher and bookseller give prejudiced advertising.

About ten years ago work with children was actively begun. Up to thirty years ago libraries were almost universally closed to children. As the modern movement gained headway it was realized that a community's collection of books is an educational tool which the librarian should administer for the greatest benefit of that community. When a librarian with this thought in mind was asked if children could borrow his library's books, only one answer was possible: that the use of a library is limited only by the number of books it contains and by the ability of the library staff to serve those who may call for them. The barriers to the admission of children to a library and to their use of its books were rapidly broken down. The age limit was dropped here and there from eighteen to twelve, then from twelve to ten, then to eight, and soon disappeared altogether.

WHAT THE LIBRARY IS DOING

As soon as children began to come with freedom to public libraries librarians discovered that they did not have a sufficient supply of books suited to children's capacities. At about this same period a change took place in the materials used in teaching reading in the public schools. Before this change, the opinion seems to have been held by school people that any material was good enough on which to practice reading. The protest which arose against this opinion resulted in the publication of a great many volumes of classic books, prepared especially for children's use. Reading in the schools came to be confined chiefly to works of writers of acknowledged merit. Pupils read, not from the old-fashioned, scrappy, graded readers, but from books called "supplementary," published especially for their edification. This movement resulted in placing on the market many hundred different books prepared for children, most of them being complete wholes from English and American literature, others being careful adaptations of classics and old myths and stories skilfully retold. This change in reading material was the beginning of an age of children's reading, in the schools as well as in public libraries.

Libraries bought these books for the young with eagerness and made them accessible to children of all classes. They soon discovered that if a library were made attractive to children and had on its shelves books within the range of their comprehension and reading power, these books would be eagerly taken and read, even though they did not include the writings of authors who had been vastly popular for several decades. To put it more plainly, the boy of twenty-five years ago wished stories by Castlemon, Optic and others of that class; but, if an inviting open-shelf library had on its shelves none of these,

159

and did have books of greater literary merit, boys would take the latter, read them with interest and pleasure, and soon would not miss their old favorites. In a word, again, libraries discovered that it was not difficult to improve, to a considerable degree, the reading taste of children in their respective communities, by the simple process of offering only the better books.

Children began to come to libraries in large numbers; in numbers too large in many cases for the single room the library could spare for their use. They not only overcrowded their special room, but their number made it impossible for librarian and assistants to give them that attention in the way of careful suggestion and specific guidance which they greatly needed.

Much was being said at this time of the importance of teaching children not simply how to read, but also what to read. More was made, perhaps, of this guidance of children in their reading than the matter deserves; or, rather, ability to read understandingly on any general subject has been found to be so important and so rare an acquisition as to put the selection of things to be read in a subordinate place.

But whether there were any call for careful guidance or not, the libraries soon realized that in their single children's room or corner they could not accommodate the crowds which came. The libraries of large towns and cities soon realized, also, the far more important fact that the crowd of young people which visited the main library was only a small portion of the children of the whole community, all of whom were equally entitled to share in the use of the public's storehouse of books.

WHAT THE LIBRARY IS DOING

The principle that a public library is for all the people, and not for the men of letters and the special student only, had by this time led to the establishment of branches. The branch idea became very popular, in some respects unduly so. It was the fashion, and the fashion has not yet quite passed, to ask a public benefactor for funds with which were built ornate and expensive structures to serve as branch libraries; structures often not well adapted to their purpose and absurdly expensive to maintain.

In these branches full half of the space available for readers was commonly given up to children. Children's departments in large city libraries thus became largely expanded, and by subdivision were made to cover, in a measure, the whole city.

The art of lending books to children now became exalted into a specialty. Children's librarians were in great demand and a school was established to train them for their work.

At this point the librarians, properly enamored of their work, but blinded a little by their enthusiasm, seemed unable to see the limits to their field, or to see the field itself in its proper relation to other educatio .al fields. They found they were popular with all children and were applauded by parents. They knew that reading is an art approved by most and that the reading of good books is approved by all. They had books under their control; they were sure they could select good ones for children, and they found the task of ministering to children's wishes a delightful one. Naturally, they hastened to increase the opportunities for this ministration. They attracted children to their special rooms in main libraries and branches by prizes, by games, by pictures, by museum specimens and by other devices.

They talked to the children, and mothered them, and read to them, and told stories to them. The art of being a librarian for children gained in importance, and, to the initiated, daily grew more recondite and more wonderful. Concerning it there developed the same group of words and phrases which accompany the growth in popularity of every new cult. The reports of meetings of children's librarians of this period, which is just coming to an end, have a very perceptible atmosphere of religious devotion, almost of fanaticism.

Especially strong was the story-telling hypnosis in this stage. It was found that children will listen to stories, and that if the stories come from books which are in the library the children, after listening to the stories, hasten to borrow the books. Here was a pleasant method of increasing the circulation and of guiding children in their reading. The discovery aroused much enthusiasm. Hundreds of young women studied the elements of dramatic art and practised on groups of children in children's rooms in libraries, that they might lead them to read more books and better ones.

This seemed to be worthy work; but it was discovered to be somewhat out of place. Story-telling has long been practised in the kindergarten as part of a well defined system. It belongs also to some extent in the first grades of the schools. To practise it in the library calls for a diversion of skill and energy from a field where skill and energy are always insufficient.

While this development of children's rooms in libraries and branches, with an accompanying development of library motherhood in the assistants, was going on, the use of books by children had been greatly encouraged by another method. It was found that, even with its branches, no library can come into close touch with more than a small per cent of all the children of the community. A library in a city of 300,000, for example, with ten distinct centers or branches, cannot get close to more than 10,000 to 20,000 of the 60,000 young people in that city. It was found, also, that no matter how skilled and enthusiastic might be the fifteen or twenty assistants in all the children's rooms of the city, their influence could reach a few individuals only.

The libraries' natural allies were obviously the teachers, and to them they turned. It would be more appropriate to say, if it could be said with truth, that the teachers turned to the libraries for assistance. But the fact is that efforts for cooperation between teachers of the art of reading and keepers of supplies of reading have come almost entirely from the latter.

Cooperation is effected chiefly in this way: The libraries lend to individual teachers small collections of books for use in their classrooms. These collections are selected by the teachers themselves, or selected by libraries for them, as the former may prefer. They include books adapted to the age and the studies of the children in the rooms to which they are sent. The teachers use them as they see fit, with no restrictions and with no financial responsibility. They may read to the class from them; they may permit the children to read from them in the room; they may lend them for home use; they may use them chiefly as a reference collection, to supplement the work done in the room; and they may change them as many times in a year, wholly or in part, as they may choose.

This seems an ideal arrangement. It puts a

163

town's or a city's collection of books at the command of the city's paid experts in education in the most complete way. It makes of every schoolroom a branch library, at no additional expense for space or service. It interests every teacher in the resources of the main library—at least it should do so. It puts a small library directly under the hand of every child in the city, and thereby tells him plainly of the large main library which is at his service. And, finally, it gives him in his reading the enthusiasm and guiding skill of one, his teacher, who should most care to persuade him to read and should have most skill in telling him what to read.

This method of sowing a library broadcast in the community is now practised in many towns and cities. It is as effective in a community scattered thinly on farms over the hills of Vermont, with its half dozen little isolated red schoolhouses, as it is in a huge school building with a score of rooms and a thousand pupils in a great city. Plainly this is a most effective and most economical way of bringing the people's books to the people's doors. It can be improved by extending the custom, already somewhat practiced, of making the collections larger, including in them books for adults and inducing teachers and pupils to work together in putting these books in the hands of the pupils' parents. The method can be supplemented by opening a room with a separate outside entrance, on the ground floor of each large city school building, as a general branch library for all who live near the building, and as a special reference library for the pupils in the buiding. This is on the point of being done in several cities.

But, effective as this classroom, branch-library method of book dissemination promises to be, it falls short in accomplishment; and its inefficiency must be laid at the door of our colleges and universities. Let me briefly explain this charge.

In our educational system stimulus and guidance come from the top. A city which has a properly equipped and efficient high school system is sure to find its primary and elementary schools well and enthusiastically conducted. A state which has a progressive university crowning its educational system finds that every high school within its borders is eager for recognition of its merits and zealous to have in fact the merits which it claims. As in efficiency and enthusiasm, so in subject and method, the highest educational institutions rule all below them.

Now, the colleges and universities of this country make of relatively small importance the arts of reading and of the use of books. Their libraries are almost without exception poorly housed. In none is there given to all pupils instruction worthy the name in the art of using a library. The students who come to them have not had persistent practice and definite instruction in the art of reading, in skill and in understanding printed words, in acquisition of a large reading vocabulary, for four or five years previous to their entering college. The importance, the fundamental and all-embracing importance, of knowledge of the English language as the vehicle of thought, as the foundation of all learning; the absolute necessity, would one become even passing wise, of being able to read good books quickly and understandingly —these things are not continually insisted upon; indeed, they are quite neglected. The colleges have lamented much that their students cannot write. It would be well if they concerned themselves first over the fact that their students cannot read.

The result of this neglect is that few college graduates know how to read. They never have been compelled to practice reading, and only by a prodigious amount of practice can any save the gifted ones ever learn to read. Also, they do not know how to use books. Also, they do not think that high skill in reading and in the art of using books and a library is the one thing of supreme importance in education.

The graduates of our colleges become teachers in high and normal schools. Their indifference to the reading art marks the work of these institutions. The result is that the teachers in our public schools, graduates of our high and normal schools, have not been made to read much; have not learned to read well; read very little during their years of teaching; know little about the literature of and for children; think that it is not of great importance that all children, by constant reading, acquire a large reading vocabulary and gain a firm hold of the tool by the use of which alone thought is possible; are indifferent to books and print; and finally, do not handle efficiently the collections they may have in their classrooms from a public library, and in many cases are not willing to have such collections.

Reading is the most important of all the arts. It is taught now chiefly through the ministrations of the yellow journals. The foundations of its proper teaching with proper and helpful material should be laid more broadly and more carefully in our colleges and universities.

THE COUNTRY CHURCH AND THE LIBRARY

Outlook, May 6, 1911

One of the chief reasons for the existence of the country church is that it promotes the happiness and efficiency—that is, the general welfare and the education and the social harmony—of the community. It should along this line, take up the work of the public library. Also, it should be the village improvement society, the federation of all study clubs for old and young, the grange, the historical museum and the museum of science and art, the chief advocate of the schools, the social center, and many other things. If it is not the head, heart, and center of all these things, it can at least be the prime mover in them and their right hand.

But, unfortunately for its efficiency in promoting general temporal welfare and spiritual well-being, it often puts too much in the foreground the restraints which religion imposes instead of the beneficent activities which it can set free.

By a happy circumstance the public library is an institution between which and the church there can be no antagonism. The library does not conflict with any doctrine. It does not interfere with the carrying out of any ceremonies, it does not represent and is not maintained by any group of people which might set it up against any church. It belongs to all members of all churches, and encourages in all that broadening of sympathies for which each and every church is proud to be thought also to stand.

The country church, if there is but one, can properly give the library a room. If this is impossible because there are rival churches, or because the one church is not approved by all of its neighbors, then it can make use of the library in a broad and helpful way.

The minister should mention it every Sunday in the year.` If new books have come in during the week, let him take them as a text for a five-minute talk. If there are no new books, let him mention three or four noteworthy articles in the magazines, or some of the older books, or a state or county publication just received and of practical value to his congregation, or a document from the United States government on forestry or birds or on some topic in agriculture locally interesting.

If the minister cannot always do this, let the librarian do it, or any one of the readers or students, old or young, in the community.

The church should not try to maintain a library of its own, but should contribute to the public library, and through its contributions should have the right to display every Sunday in its main meeting-room a few good books for old and young. To these some one should allude during the service every Sunday, and then those who wished could look them over and take home what they selected.

If there is no library, the church should establish one, or see to it that one is established. How to do this there are many who are able and willing to tell.

If the one church, or the several churches, of the community make it known that a public library is to be set up in the town, or if they make it known that the library already established is to be warmly supported and freely used by the churches, the progress of the scheme cannot well be slow. Friends, publishers, magazine editors, secretaries of societies for the promotion of education in agriculture, forestry, art, village improvement, and many other topics will send in publications.

If churches and the library unite, the efficiency of both will be greatly increased. In any specific community, if the exact social, religious, and educational conditions are known, it should be easy to give specific suggestions along certain lines of work; and though the remarks above are quite general, I am sure that if they meet with approval in any country community the people of the church in that community will have no difficulty in carrying out certain definite and helpful plans.

As every one knows, the country church is now the social center of its own members, the point about which many interests gather already. If to those interests there is added the work which can be done for and by and through the books, periodicals, pictures, and the librarian of a public library, then the church's work will be much broader and more helpful still. Moreover, through its work with and for a public library, which grows out of and belongs to the whole community more fully than does any church, the church will broaden in the best way its own interests and its own feelings and its own powers.

WOMEN IN LIBRARY WORK

Independent, August 3, 1911

Of all occupations now open to women, work in a public library is perhaps the most attractive. This is not because the money return is large, for in this respect both teaching and clerical work have the advantage. Library work is attractive because it gives one pleasant surroundings, brings one into contact with intelligent people, helps one to keep abreast of the times, is not often unduly severe or trying to the nerves, and offers openings for many kinds of native talent to show themselves at their best.

A public library is the property of the people who use it. The librarian recognizes this fact and tries to make this school of the people as attractive and as pleasing as possible. If a public institution is to be inviting and helpful, those who work in it and for it must be interested in it, must wish it to gain in popularity and must be proud of its good repute. Now, a library's staff cannot have for it the feelings just mentioned unless they themselves find in it and in their work for it a certain pleasure, and enjoy in it a certain good fellowship with one another. As they are to one another, so, in large measure, will they appear to those who call at the library for books or for opportunities for reading and study. Within a library, therefore, must be found the free cooperative spirit of the home. The presence in a library of this feeling of good will and helpfulness is alone almost enough to explain its popularity as a place in which to earn one's living; and when we add to this element of attractiveness the other factors already mentioned and especially the one I shall try especially to describe, it is easy to understand why library work appeals so strongly to so many women. This special point of advantage which library work offers lies in the many kinds of employment it includes and the many kinds of talent and skill to which it appeals.

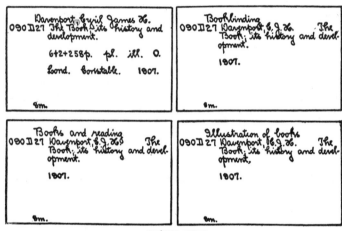

CATALOG CARDS

Let me make my meaning plain. Do you have some skill with the pen, can you write clearly, are you painstaking and accurate and can you follow exactly rules set for your guidance? Then, even though you are not distinctly bookish, you may find a place as a subordinate in a library's catalog department. If you add, to the modest talents mentioned, skill as typewriter, then you may still more easily find here a place. You would write cards like those shown above. From two to twenty of these cards are written for every book which a library adds to its shelves. In writing or copying these cards you can learn, if you will, and almost without effort, something about the best books of to-day and of all time.

WOMEN IN LIBRARY WORK

Have you a good knowledge of books and skill in discovering quickly what are the main points in any volume you may pick up? To a good general education do you add a logical or at least an orderly mind? You may, then, after proper study and discipline, find a place in a library as a classifier. To classify books for the library is so to mark them that when they are arranged on the shelves in the numerical or alphabetical order of the marks and symbols you put on them, they will fall into groups; books of the same subject standing together, and groups on the same subject standing near other groups on allied subjects. Properly to add books to a library already classified, a library let us say of 50,000 volumes, so that one who wishes to consult them may readily find the ones he seeks, is a task calling for skill and common sense. It is work many women have learned to do well.

In preparing the originals of the records of books added to a library, making of the records an index called the card catalog, other special qualities are called for. Especially does the worker in this line need a large fund of sympathy with other minds, quick appreciation of how the average person of intelligence will approach a subject. A library's catalog is a dictionary of world knowledge; it is, rather, an index to such a dictionary, the dictionary being found in the thousands of books on the library shelves. Skill in making such an index seems almost native to some of the women in our libraries.

The kinds of work thus far mentioned call for some general education, for long special practice or for peculiar aptness or for all three. But, in the same department in which the things last mentioned are carried out much other work of clerical nature is also

173

done. If you are without much book knowledge but are patient, careful, accurate and skilful with your hands, you may find work in a library in this subordinate department of the library's index making. For example, in almost every library a book must be looked over before it is put on the shelf to see that it is complete, and, if its leaves are unopened, they must be carefully cut. This latter task alone is no light one. An active young woman can do little more than cut the pages of six or seven hundred volumes in a week's time of forty to fifty hours.

In every book there must be pasted, inside the front cover, a book plate; if it is a lending book, there must be pasted in the back a pocket; on this pocket, usually a blank piece of paper, certain symbols or words must be written; a book card must be prepared, to be kept in the book when it is on the shelf and to be retained in the library when the book is lent to show to whom it was lent; on the back of the book must be put a label.

If you have always been a reader, and by a reader I mean one who has seized the spare moments to devour books, papers and journals from the time she was six until she was, let us say, twenty-two; and if you remember what you read; if you have an agreeable presence and know how to say "no" as pleasantly as "yes," yet tend to be obliging rather than the opposite, then you might find a place as an assistant at the lending desk of a library. Here the public calls for books and here an attendant, getting them from the shelves, delivers them. The routine is not simple. Modern libraries believe so strongly that the fewest possible difficulties should be put in the way of borrowers and the fewest possible duties laid on them, that they tend naturally to throw upon the attendant at the lending desk a large amount of detail. The chief of the lending department of a large library must be a person of very decided genius. You cannot aspire to such a position unless you have either a college education or its equivalent, a wide knowledge of books, no small experience in life, agreeable manners, and ability to meet people of all ranks on their own level. The routine is done by people who are not thus well equipped.

Have you read much in many lines? Is your memory retentive? Do books seem to you to have individualities and to be distinct from one another like so many human beings? Does a moment's glance at a book fix its general features in your memory? Do you feel almost instinctively what a book, and especially an encyclopedia or any other work of reference, can tell you? Then you may hope to do good work, though perhaps only after some years of practice, in a reference department. To the person who delights in knowledge, and instinctively takes in and retains information of all kinds, and never forgets in which book a fact was found, to such a person general reference work especially appeals. Not a few women have some special talent along this line and may hope to find interesting occupation here.

Book surgery, book hygiene and book rebinding form a department of library work which was long neglected, but is now seen to be of great importance. Any woman who is clever with her hands and does not scorn manual labor could make herself useful in this department. In large libraries the head of the binding and repair department must be a person who knows and can answer questions like these, about any of the thousands of wounded books which come to her for attention: "Is it still popular, and should it therefore be rebound?" "Is it so trivial that it is not worth even an hour's work of mending?" "Tho old and worn, is it a book the library should always have on its shelves?" "Is it a book-rarity, which should be carefully mended and then as carefully rebound?" "Is its paper so poor that to rebind it is a waste of money?"

A knowledge of book-making and literature such as these queries suggest is not all the head of this department must have. She must know about leather, cloth, paper, string, tape, thread, glue, paste and many other things which go to the making, repairing and rebinding of books; and she must also know enough about the binder's craft to be able to tell whether a book is skillfully and honestly rebound or not.

In many public libraries a third of all the books taken to homes are lent to children. The children have rooms of their own in most libraries; and here, if you are fond of children and have some tact in their management, you may hope to find a place. The work is not easy, but is not as trying as teaching. If you hope to make progress in it you must be a reader, as I have already defined the word, and especially you must know the books which children read and the books about children. Moreover, this children's work brings one in contact with the schools, and to be effective here one must know something about the teacher's work, her difficulties, her classroom conditions, her textbooks and her courses of study.

The kinds of work I have mentioned are done in separate and semi-independent departments in larger libraries. In some of them it is the custom to test the capacity, taste and skill of each new member of the staff, particularly of those not trained in any other library, by placing them in several departments in succession until the work they are best fitted for is found.

In the smallest library all the kinds of work I have mentioned and many other kinds also, as well as many minor details, are done by one or two persons and it is in the small library that a young woman can find the best opportunity to show her capacity for work helpful to the community which supports her library; and an opportunity also to gain a broad general education and admirable training in the special field of library economy.

There is no public institution quite as broad in its possibilities of public service as the free public library in America, and especially the free library of the small town.

The library worker in such a library, if she has the wisdom and temperament proper for her position, does not need a great store of book knowledge when she begins, nor does she need great skill in the technique of her calling; for she will necessarily acquire these things if she performs her duties well and tries to take advantage of all opportunities. She must be a friend of her trustees, their adviser and their business manager; she must watch the funds and practice economy yet not permit her community to think about the library in terms of parsimony; she must select and buy the books best suited to her town and she is the person who, if she is fit for her position, can do this to the best advantage, better than any book committee can do it. She must meet with and make friends of all patrons, old and young, and be their adviser in matters both serious and recreational concerning reading; she must attract the teachers that through them she may reach the children; she must lead the children themselves from nickel libraries or, what is more difficult, from no reading whatever, to the good things in print for them, and the children must not know they are being led; she must know about women's clubs, and help form their programs and buy books that will be useful to their members; and she must not forget boys' debating societies, and lyceum lectures, and special duties in churches and in Sunday schools, and questions of village improvement, like sewers and sidewalks and trees and water supply; and she must be interested in all other things that concern her town, and ready to supply the book or journal that gives the latest and best information about them. The history of the town, the soil, the products, the climate, the geography, the industries, the fairs, the games, the festivals—all these she must keep in her mind as matters which may any day prove of special interest and may demand special information. A historical society, or a science museum, or a nature club, or a farmer's club may any day spring into life, and it will then be her pleasure to furnish some encouragement and much information to those interested.

I have set down thus briefly the wide variety of work which may fall to the lot of the librarian of the small library, because all of these kinds of work are found also in the larger libraries, are there much specialized and may there attract, as this paper tries to show, women of very varied gifts and accomplishments.

To go a little further with the librarian of the modest town and thus, though indirectly, with the humblest or the highest assistant in the large library. The outside world must not absorb her; for she must know her books. To know them she must read unceasingly; not much in a few books, but a little in all the books, all the journals, all the book catalogs, all the many pamphlets and all the newspapers which come to her library. With her there can be no question of what to read; she must read it all; not all of all she sees, but a little of everything she sees. Any worker in any library who does not read, read, read, and forever read, can not hope for and ought not to expect any notable success.

What this friend of books who has books in her charge and learns to know them and learns to know her town—what this modest librarian does for her community by the agency of her library and its books is another story. My purpose in this paper is simply to show that to work among a library's books for the people who own the books is a many-sided occupation, attractive through its general character to all right-minded young women, and appealing specially to women of varied tastes and talents through its many-sidedness.

BRANCH LIBRARIES IN SCHOOL HOUSES

*Address Delivered before the American Library
Institute, September, 1911*

Two very important changes are rapidly taking
place in the management of public schools. One is
the adoption of the plan of all-the-year sessions. Up
to about five years ago it was impossible to find in
the educational literature of this country any mention, much less any discussion, of the subject of the
short school year, the long vacation and the frequent
holiday and their influence on public school efficiency. To-day the situation is greatly changed.
All-the-year schools are freely discussed and very
generally advocated. Except for an accident this
system would have been given a trial in two large
schools in Newark this year. Several smaller towns
are already testing it; some of the Cleveland high
schools have adopted it; and the admission is now
freely made that the present short and badly broken
educational year of 189 days is one of the most
serious of the burdens under which our schools are
suffering. The adoption of this rational school year
will mean the use of city public school buildings by
day schools for about 250 days each year instead of
the present 189.

This increase in the days in which school buildings are in use is of great interest to the library
profession. It is quite in line with the effect of the
second of the two noteworthy changes in public
school management which, as I have said, are now
under way, that is, the growth of the use of school
buildings by the general public.

This appropriation by the people of their own
school buildings to public purposes has perhaps been

carried further in Rochester, N. Y., than anywhere else. The fame of what has there been done has been very admirably and very helpfully spread abroad. A like movement has been going on in many other towns and cities. Only those who can recall the universal hostility with which was received twenty years ago, the suggestion that school houses be used for general educational and social purposes, can realize how great has been the revolution in public opinion in this respect. Within a few years no city will plan a school building without providing for its use by those who live near it in a score of helpful, social ways, no one of which would have have been thought, twenty years ago, to be part of the functions of such a structure.

Add, now, to the all-the-year use of school houses by daylight public schools, their use on Saturdays, vacations and evenings by the parents of the pupils, and you have a building very much better suited to be the home of a branch library—and in the small community of the public library itself—than was the school house of a few years ago.

Another quite recent development of public school work makes the school building a still better center for a library. I refer to the evening school, which flourishes in every large city and in many has grown to enormous proportions. Newark is in the front rank among American cities in the number of pupils in its evening schools and in the proportion of attendance to enrollment. Last winter there were eighteen elementary evening schools, six evening high schools, an evening drawing school, an evening technical school, with a total enrollment in all of them of 14,800 students; this in a city of 340,000 population.

In the public school building of to-morrow we shall

have a day school in session nearly 250 days per year, and an evening school in session probably two-thirds as many evenings; adults will have in it every evening and on many holiday afternoons lectures, socials, debates, special classes in domestic science, hygiene and a score of other things.

It is self-evident that in a public building thus used there should be a branch of the public library. A building thus used, moreover, provides nearly all the social center facilities which at one time the branch library, or the main library itself, seemed alone fitted to furnish.

The conclusion is inevitable, that a city's branch libraries will in the future find their proper locations in most cases in that city's school buildings.

It is not necessary to raise here the argument of economy. It may, and probably will, cost less to equip and maintain branch libraries in school houses than in independent buildings; but unless the branch in the school house were more efficient and generally better adapted to its ends than the independent branch, the change of location would not be justified. A very brief consideration of the matter makes it seem almost self-evident that a branch library in the school house of the new type will be in the most strategic quarters that can be found for it.

The ideal building of the future, to indulge in a forecast based on many actual approximations to an ideal, will contain school rooms used for kindergartens, for ordinary schools, and for manual or vocational training, and at night for evening schools of many kinds. It will also contain a gymnasium, large and small assembly rooms with stages, lanterns, curtains, etc., cooking and domestic economy equipment, equipment for freehand and mechanical drawing, museum room, and a library. This library will have an outside entrance and will be open at all hours, not only for teachers and pupils, but also for the people of the neighborhood. On the special arrangement and equipment of this room I need not here enlarge.

The trend of educational development is toward this wider and fuller use of public buildings and toward this closer cooperation between the directors of formal education and the keepers of the people's books.

The arrangement just described will probably not lead to the disappearance of the branch library as an offshoot of a main central independent institution, even if the branch be in a school house. The advantages which accrue to the community from the possession of a library with its own management and its own individuality seem to be too great to be given up for the sake of a possible reduction of expense. Branch libraries in the schools will probably continue to be parts of an independent library system.

But toward such a cooperation and combination of the library and the public school as I have briefly outlined it would seem that we are steadily moving.

The use of public school buildings for many purposes for which, up to a very recent date, they were assumed not to be adapted, is but one special aspect of the recent rapid growth of municipal efficiency. Our cities have, as might be expected in a new country, failed to govern themselves well. This failure has shown itself in many ways, and particularly in the lack of cooperation between departments. This lack has led to much duplication of labor, doubling of expense and neglect of important work that gained nobody's attention because it seemed everybody's business. Some cities, for example, have had three sets of summer playgrounds provided respectively by a board of education, a park and shade tree commission and a special commission on playgrounds.

The educational work of a community includes day schools, evening schools, trade and vocational schools, playgrounds, summer schools, libraries, museums of art, science and technology, and many other things. The well-governed city of the future may find it wise to group all these educational movements under one management. Whether that will be the best possible plan, no one as yet can tell. It is quite plain, however, that much closer cooperation will be insisted on than has heretofore been practiced between the bodies which manage a city's efforts to teach and train its youth. It is toward this helpful cooperation that school and library move when they unite in placing in each school building an ample and well-managed collection of the world's best books.

RELATIONS OF A LIBRARY TO ITS CITY

Address Delivered before the League of American Municipalities, Buffalo, September 18, 1912

I seem to find myself constitutionally opposed to the office-holder. We all have our sinful thoughts and perhaps this is mine! Through one of life's little jokes I am an office-holder myself, partly, one might suppose, in punishment for my sinfulness of thought. Through another of life's little jokes the punishment does not fit the criminal, since I thoroughly enjoy my office-holding! For over twenty years I have found that I leave my library with regret, however long the day has been, and return to it always with delight.

This anti-office-holding theory is simple and axiomatic. A man conducting his own business wins money, fame and honor by attention, toil, integrity and brains; and loses money, fame and honor through negligence, sloth, double-dealing and stupidity. A man conducting a public business finds that excellence of work may sometimes accompany him direct to the pillory of condemnation by his master the voter, and that work evilly done may sometimes go with high public favor. The man who runs a business finds that success waits chiefly on his own efforts; the man in the public office finds that success waits on voters' whims. The man in business cultivates his business; the man in office must cultivate his constituents. The business man is driven to efficiency, the office-holder is driven to dally with the voter!

There you have in brief the theory under which we find that a democracy of offices and elections is condemned to submit to inefficient holders of office

187

And yet, here we are, and doing not so ill as the theory says we must. Perhaps the theory grants not enough to the factor of poor human nature. Perhaps human nature compels some of us to enjoy our tasks and to do our best in them, regardless of tumult and shouting at the primaries and astounding conclusions at the ballot-box.

A friend in Newark who is but a close second and almost a first with me in enthusiasm for democratic ideals, is fond of saying that after all public business is more honestly managed than a great private business; perhaps not as effectively managed,—an overplus of rotation in office is alone sufficient to prevent that,—but more decently and with less financial waste.

I find it hard to believe him. Governmental sins are so obtrusive, are so hilariously dangled before us by an unterrified public press.

But, in these later years I begin to see facts that weigh heavily on his side. Here is one. A great railroad spent a few millions in improving its line. Under certain huge embankments it built arches for the passage of highways. Against due warnings, intent more on immediate economies than on community welfare or the voice of forethought, it built these arches narrower than the state law commanded. Now it must spend about half a million dollars in rebuilding and widening these same arches! Somewhere in that railroad's management is a spirit which is at times self-centered and pig-headed and here, for one of its demonstrations, the stockholders must meekly pay a sum large enough to arouse a noble tumult among the voters—were their city fathers to make a like error—of the largest municipality.

And so, at sight of an example here and there of excellence in office, easily found if you look, and of stupidity and sin in plain and pure business, I become reconciled to my position as a delighted, somewhat laborious and I hope moderately successful office holder.

As such it is a pleasure to meet with my fellows who are seeking to learn from one another so much of the fine and difficult art of city management as each may have discovered. If we must be municipal officials, let us do our best to learn the art and craft of public business.

Other trades, arts and sciences less difficult than city management have their clubs, leagues and associations and pass the hat for contributions of ideas for the common purse of information. Then let managers of cities also join hands. In this business there is much to learn and nothing to conceal. There are no trade secrets in civics. The jealousies of size and beauty are for promoters and real estate speculators and are always squelched at last by health reports and census figures. In city government you can establish no monopoly of excellence. You may use a patent pavement if you are in the patent pavement stage of development; but the art of cheaply keeping it clean is not open to patent or copyright.

The fact is that the world knows how to run a city in the best possible way. The world knows it, but no one man knows it and no one city knows it. I mean that somewhere in this or other lands, some mayor, fire or police commissioner, health officer, school supervisor or what not is running his particular department better than it was ever run before, more easily, more cheaply, more agreeably to the public.

It is our business to find him, get from him his method, always given for the asking, and apply it.

189

The best in every line, that is what this league is seeking for and wishing to apply. The city that finds and applies these best ideas is the city that is best governed. A league devoted to the search for the world's best municipal ideas is a league to encourage.

Here is where the library comes in. In books, journals and reports, that is, in print, are to be found all of these best ideas, and if you wish to find them to print you must go. Now, it is a library's business to take care of all that's in print, to store it and index it and so fix it that it will yield up to the inquirer all that it contains. In print somewhere are nearly all the secrets of good city management.

Your first library should be your own. You have already accepted the idea of a central bureau of municipal knowledge; you could do no better thing than to carry out the idea in all its fullness. Every city needs the expert, not now and then but at every turn. The expert is simply one who has cast an unprejudiced eye on many actual experiments and drawn the obvious conclusion therefrom. A library of municipal reports is a collection of municipal experiences. Gather these reports and put by them men able to draw from them the facts and to set the facts in good order, and expertness comes forth. In Newark we ignorantly quarrel over the paving of our Broad street. Your league library should send us, for a reasonable fee, the results of the latest experiments in paving of every kind under conditions like our own, and our quarrel would be at once relieved of ignorance and reduced to dollars and cents.

Every librarian in the country, every city government, every expert and every contractor for city work would welcome a great library founded by a league of cities. Whatever it might cost it would earn that cost a hundred times over every year. Consider the countless letters and circulars every intelligent city department is every year paying for to get information from other cities, information which is always fragmentary and usually misleading. A league library would tell the whole story and tell it straight to a hundred cities at once at little more than the present cost of incomplete information to one.

Consider also the endless errors of judgment into which cities fall through lack of the latest information on sewage, fire prevention, construction, administration and a hundred other things, all costing money, often very much money, and nearly all avoidable with the aid of a great central bureau of municipal knowledge and municipal experiences.

But you are familiar with all this, and have begun the work indicated. I speak of it because as a librarian I realize how valuable a really great bureau would be and how gladly it would be welcomed and eagerly cooperated with by all the progressive public libraries in the country.

Of this league library the municipal library of every city would be a branch. Much of the work municipal libraries now vainly attempt to do would be better done by that of the league. But each city would still have its own problems, peculiar to itself, in the solution of which its own library would be most helpful. Moreover, every city must keep its own records with increasing care and must, if it is to legislate wisely, change its ordinances and draft new ones in the light of information which a municipal library, complete, well indexed and controlled by a master of books and print can alone furnish.

The institution I have charge of is a free public library. It was established in 1889. Its building was erected on vote of the citizens and at their own expense in 1900, at a cost of $325,000 and among all in the country which are at all like it in size or cost is easily the best. I was not in Newark when it was built so I speak without prejudice; I have worked in it for eleven years and have seen many other libraries, so I speak with knowledge; I am rather proud of good things in my adopted city, so I speak with pleasure; and as I now have the floor, I can speak without fear of immediate contradiction.

The building being of the best, the institution it houses should enjoy a like degree of excellence. Here I am more modest in my expression and will confine myself to saying that Newark seems to like it.

An ounce of experience is worth a pound of theory, so instead of trying to describe to you the place an ideal library occupies in the life of an ideal city I am going to tell you very briefly what the Newark library has been and done in its city in the years I have known its work, since January, 1901. Were there more time I would depart from my story now and then to tell of certain good things other libraries have done which we have not, for there are other libraries; and you will pretend to be reasonably surprised, I hope, when I say that some have done things we have not, or have done better what we have also done.

But first let me give you an axiom or two. Public institutions should enjoy the approval, the respect and, I dare to use the word, the affection of their public. Do you inquire about the place of any city department in the life of its city? Go find if the public like it and are proud of it, and your question is answered. It is an axiom, is it not? And it applies, does it not, as well to the private enterprise working within a city as surely and entirely as it does to any city department? How much more comfortable, efficient and prosperous many a public utility business would have been in the past decade had they pasted that axiom in their hats, and then lived up to it!

Now, I think Newark likes its public library and have faith she is proud of it. Two things lead me to these conclusions and lend me the conceit to say them:

First, the generous hospitality with which I have been treated in all my eleven years of residence. I think they were proud of their library when I came, and they had reason to be if only because they built it and paid for it themselves, and quite naturally they expected it to continue to be worthy and enjoyable and to have at its head one whom they could pleasantly endure. At any rate, there the good will was, and I defy any man of feeling to go to a new city and be received with good will and good wishes and hearty support, as I was, and not put forth his best in the effort to make his work a success. I hope these remarks are not too personal!

Another reason for thinking Newarkers like their library is that they support it. Our annual income has grown in eleven years from $44,000 to $120,000, nearly threefold and it is difficult to find those who have begrudged the money. Following the axiom I gave you, is another, that if you like a thing you are willing to pay what it costs.

Our library was established in 1889. For twelve years it was well but very modestly housed in an old remodeled theatre. It got its second wind, and almost a new birth when it moved into its building twelve years ago. It is the story of its eleven latest years, during which I have known it intimately, that I shall tell you.

In 1901 we had 79,000 books and Newark people took home to read 315,000 a year; we now have 200,000 and this year we lend over a million.

Now, those are the basic figures of most estimates of libraries. And it is true that the good library grows in books and is more used by its patrons every year. But conditions so vary in different cities that these figures never tell the whole story. Newark is not a reading city. It is industrial, it is a suburb, and thousands of its adults speak English only a little and read it not at all. To promote the library's use we had to advertise it, and in advertising we spent much energy, time and money. The trustees said, in effect, "Our city has put into this plant, including land, building, equipment and books, about three-quarters of a million dollars. If this plant is idle that money is locked up and doesn't even draw interest. The people of our town don't know what a good thing their public library is, and it is our duty to show them and get them to use it." And they did; and the story of how they did is the story of the library's work over and above the buying, indexing and lending of books.

One of the mysteries of modern library management is the pay roll. To explain that mystery is not my business today. I will only say that our pay roll takes about 53 per cent of our income, and that is the average in all the larger libraries of the country right now. This means that our library has been able to take a place in the city's life, besides buying and lending books, without spending more on salaries than do libraries which are not so municipally active.

Our building is so large that we still have seven

194

rooms, having a total of more than 10,000 square feet, which the book part of our work doesn't need.

We have had some or all of the building open for public use every day in eleven years save about twenty-five; a total of 50 per cent more hours than any other public building in the city, and more than three times as many hours as the school houses. I maintain that this is as it should be. A public building should be used. While the building was thus open the people of the city held in the spare rooms mentioned, in eleven years, about 6,000 meetings, by and for nearly 700 different organizations, with a total attendance of about 180,000. These meetings ranged from boys' debating clubs to the Board of Trade, and covered such subjects as city planning, charity, hospitals, pedagogy, tuberculosis, philosophy, languages, and the world's peace. As long as there was a room unused any public welfare educational movement, not looking for money profits to any individual, could find free of charge for its orderly meetings a warm, well-lighted and properly janitored room in the library building. On many days ten such meetings have been held. In this movement for getting the maximum of use out of a city's public educational buildings I wish to make here a claim for Newark as pioneer in liberality and extent. Of disturbance, bad feeling, trouble, because the A's could have a room for their meetings and the B's could not —of this kind of thing there was in the eleven years not an item worthy of mention.

We call this daily use of the library plant very good advertising. While it has been going on the annual use of the library's books increased about 300 per cent while the population increased about 40 per cent.

LIBRARIES

I said Newark is not a reading town. It seemed the library's business to try to make it one. Grownups can't be taught to use books. Children can; so we put a good deal of time, thought and money into plans for introducing school children to good books.

In eleven years teachers have taken into their school rooms more than 5,000 little libraries of about fifty books each, kept them for a term and used them to encourage and guide the reading of their pupils. We have children's books in most of our branches, and we have a room for children in the library building, and about a fourth of the million books we lend each year are borrowed by young people.

We wanted to help interest the children in their city, so we began about ten years ago to gather interesting books, articles, clippings and pictures on Newark. Then we induced a newspaper man who knew his own city to write a history of Newark for young people, and we published it. Then Newark study began to creep into the public school course, and we continued to hunt up and reprint and lend short accounts of Newark institutions of all kinds, city departments, public buildings, parks, streets, trolleys, trees, water, sewage, hospitals, and scores of other things. Then the schools supplied themselves with better maps of the city, about ten feet square, than any city school had ever had before; then the Board of Education asked an assistant superintendent to write a course of study on Newark for all the grades—and he did, and so we have the first carefully worked out and by far the most complete plan for teaching the children of a city to know their own city that the world has yet seen.

Please put down this my second claim for Newark, that she is the pioneer in teaching children city patriotism in the only rational way, by giving them, first, a knowledge of their city and so an intelligent interest in their city and, thereby, sympathy with their city, and, therefore, a wish to help their city to become more prosperous, better governed, clean, more beau· tiful and a more attractive place to live in.

The library's share of all this work was also adver· tising, at least we called it so, and it paid.

You know Newark has begun all-year schools in two of its biggest buildings; this being one of the first and the most successful trials of the plan. I was in one of the classrooms in August and found the children reciting a lesson on the story of our water supply from sheets of information the library had furnished. By and by we must spend a few millions more on our water plant. Those children will surely take an intelligent interest in the question.

Some one asked if any of the class used library books. Nearly every hand went up. This was in the Italian quarter.

Teachers are not yet well trained in the high and normal schools and colleges, which they attend while getting their equipment as pedagogues, to know chil· dren's books or to use a library. So we wrote text· books on these two subjects and have been giving our normal school students a short course on the latter, this year to 120 students, and are just about to give a course to the older students on the former. Some day all normal schools will themselves do these things; few do it yet. We do it because we think it good advertising, in the long run. The students go into the schools as teachers and in turn teach the children to use good books—the library's books and all others—and to use them to their profit.

All our work with young people is managed from

a special department which has a room and a sort of a bureau of information for teachers in the main library building.

Teachers need pictures in this pictorial age, and we have nearly 500,000 in the library, arranged like a huge pictorial dictionary under subjects, with 40,000 of them conveniently mounted and displayed, besides 800 big colored pictures, large enough to be seen across a school room, to decorate the walls and to illustrate subjects of study. Teachers borrow the smaller ones by tens of thousands and the larger by scores.

In one of our high schools we have a library and a skilled librarian. It is one of the best institutions of its kind in the country. We expect to have similar libraries in our two new high schools and in our normal school's new building. Also we expect to have libraries for community use in many of our school buildings just as soon, and that will be very soon, as the world accepts to the full the axiom that a public building should be always in use.

For the high schools we print pamphlet lists of good books, compiled by the teachers, for the pupils to select their required reading from every term, and we supply the books. I have brought a few of the lists. We are almost as proud of them as the high schools are.

The city did not ask anyone to give it a library; but built it for and by itself. That is one reason why it is so good, so we think. It does not wish to ask for the gift of branch library buildings, so all our branches are in rented storerooms, on main business streets, and are small, simple, and very effective. Later we hope to build two or three branches to be used also as civic centers. We lend as many books from some of these little stores, which the people seem to think are just as inviting as palaces built with an outsider's money, as are lent from any elaborate structures costing $100,000 and over. They advertise us very well.

The library building was the first piece of good architecture the city ever put up for itself. It looked so well and served so good a purpose and set so good an example that since it was finished in 1900 the people have voted for a good city hall, a very good and absolutely untainted city hall, a good court house, good fire stations, good schools and other good things in architecture. One of the notable things the library did, in the life of this particular town, was to set an excellent and very practical example in city architecture.

To adorn the building within—it is very simply decorated—we now and then bought a picture, a vase, a piece of bronze or marble. Generous citizens added to the collection. In our spare rooms we began to hold loan exhibitions of art objects, displays of school work, industrial exhibits, modest Newark history exhibits. Some one gave us a fine collection of minerals, rocks, soils, building stones, economic plants, etc. Then it seemed wise to form a Museum Asso ᐧ ation, for which the city bought a collection of ar⁺ objects which we had borrowed to show, and almost before we knew it we had art and science museum⌄. well established, modest and yet possessing already more than $40,000 worth of property, growing rapidly, all housed in the library's spare rooms, and properly called its offspring. Soon they will be so large as to need a building of their own, which the city will surely furnish.

These exhibitions I spoke of numbered over

seventy-five in the eleven years and drew over 300,000 visitors to the library, so we called them also good advertising.

I said that nearly all good municipal ideas are somewhere in print. The same is true of business information and of nearly all good business ideas. We thought the library ought to try to gather this information and these ideas and make them accessible to the people who are making Newark what it is, manufacturers, merchants, and men engaged in insurance, commerce, engineering and what not. So we established in a rented room, on the ground floor, on the principal office street, near the center of the city, what we call a business branch. No other public library in the country has yet offered so conveniently to its public so good a collection of maps, business and trade directories and books and pamphlets on manufacturing and trade and business affairs as we have there. Yet it is only in its infancy.

We hope to produce here in time a library which will fit the needs of "the Newark that does things" just as closely as your league library will in time fit the needs of every municipality. We have made an index of things made in Newark, naming 1,200 different firms and telling what firms make 4,000 different objects. Some day we hope to print it. Now it is on cards and open for use. To get this information we sent out several thousand letters to Newark citizens who are makers of things.

This advertised the practical, business side of our resources very well; but still did not bring about as great a use of our material as it deserved. So we decided to publish a journal, a monthly, and call it the Newarker, and to have it, as its advertisements said, "introduce a city to itself and to its public library." We have run it almost a year. It has articles on many aspects of the city life, with interesting maps and illustrations. It is in a measure a "municipal journal," though run as yet by one part of the city organization only. We hope through it to reach ultimately a good many of the men of our city who seem to think their public library is only for readers of novels, philosophy, art and literature, and not for men of affairs. I think we shall succeed. In any event we shall have done another bit of advertising of the kind that is sure to pay in the long run.

I have brought for your inspection a few copies of this Newarker, which you are welcome to take away.

THE PUBLIC LIBRARY AND PUBLICITY IN MUNICIPAL AFFAIRS

Paper Read before the New York Library Club, March 13, 1913

On this subject I have no theories to advance, save this very general one, to which I assume all librarians give assent:

"The librarian of a public library is that servant of the community who has in charge sources of information—books and journals of utility—as well as works of art in the form of books of literature. These sources of information should be such as furnish facts about the town or city which supports the library; not its history only, by any means, but present-day facts on subjects like character of population, industries, educational facilities, water supply and sanitary conditions. The books and journals of facts should include also statements from experts on problems of town development, like those of paving, street layout, policing, fire protection, improvement of water supply and extension of educational facilities."

If the theory thus briefly stated is sound, then every public library should have been a bureau of municipal information and municipal research and a general storehouse of civic knowledge long before the so-called municipal library was ever mentioned. So much for what librarians should have done and did not do.

Perhaps one of the most difficult problems Americans are facing to-day is that of how to manage towns and cities. There is no short-cut to the solution of this problem. New methods of election, new forms of ballot, new kinds of primaries, commission government—these alleged remedies are not remedies at all. The only sure cure for social inefficiency is increase of intelligence and good will.

A city's public library tries to help this much-needed growth of intelligence and good will. Librarians have usually taken on faith the doctrine that to read the world's great books is to grow in grace and social excellence, and have been satisfied if, through their activities, they increased in their respective communities the amount of use made of good literature. Special emphasis has been placed by them on the salutary effect on the American people of acquaintance with the world's classics. Now, I am skeptical of the value of acquaintance with the classics as an education in good citizenship or as an incentive thereto. I believe there is more inspiration to civic decency for a child in the story of how his community gets a supply of pure water than there is in the best fairy tale ever devised or the noblest Teutonic myth ever born.

A child can be taught to worship, in a measure, the heroes of another country and another time; but that worship will not lead him to refrain from sweeping the dirt from the sidewalk in front of his tenement into the street gutter. After imitation and habit—and he finds in most American cities few to imitate and still fewer to help him to good habits in civic cleanliness—the strongest impulse to consider his city's good looks and general well-being is knowledge of the why and wherefore of affairs, like sidewalks, streets, gutters and the cost of street cleaning.

Good will toward the community and the wish to serve it are born of acquaintance with it, just as affection for one's friends and a desire to help them are born of close intimacy.

Basing our work on this theory, we have in Newark been able, largely through the influence of the public library, to put to the front a very elaborately conceived and elaborately equipped enterprise for publicity in municipal affairs.

The method was as follows: Beginning ten years ago, the library accumulated municipal information. This information, if not already in suitable form for young people's use, it digested and arranged and simplified and issued on sheets for general use, and especially for the use of children. With the help of teachers, an interest in this information was aroused among many of the school pupils. Municipal affairs were used as topics for study, essay and discussion.

This work went on for several years, increasing slowly in extent all the time. Finally it took definite shape at the hands of the educational authorities. There was then published, in 1912, a "Course of study on the city of Newark," for use in all the schools of the city, from the first to the eighth grade, written by Mr. J. Wilmer Kennedy, assistant superintendent of public schools. This was the first complete thing of its kind, so far as my knowledge goes, in the history of public education. Accompanying the "Course" itself, were many supplementary leaflets and appropriate maps.

We look upon this as the most valuable contribution to publicity in municipal affairs that the Newark Library has had anything to do with. Only time will tell whether, being pushed in the schools, it will produce the effect hoped for.

LIBRARIES

If it is successful, all future generations of Newarkers will, in their very childhood, begin to learn their city; will know how it has grown, why it has grown as it has, what it has accomplished, in what it has failed, what it needs, and how the things it needs can best be obtained. Being thus informed, they will not only vote intelligently once a year, but will also act intelligently, and with some affection for the city, on every one of the 364 days between elections.

The titles of the topics in this course of study and of the accompanying leaflets will help one to understand its scope and character. A few of them are: Literary landmarks of Newark, Men and women of Newark, Juvenile courts, Shade trees and parks, Noise in cities, Transportation, Milk supply, Playgrounds.

A somewhat different form of publicity in public and quasi-public affairs has been carried on for several years in our main library, but more especially in what we call our Business Branch. At this branch we not only keep on hand the kinds of information and the kinds of literature that we are using in our campaign for the promotion of city interest among young people; we have also collected there a large mass of material having to do with what may be called the private interests of Newark citizens, their business affairs.

On the municipal or governmental side, we include the publications of the city of Newark, the county of Essex and the state of New Jersey, the publications of a good many other cities on those subjects in which Newark is just now particularly interested, and many publications of state and national governments. Maps of all kinds supplement this material, especially maps of Newark and Essex

206

county, showing highways, trolley lines, water supply, sewage equipment, fire stations, police stations, schools, voting districts and scores of other things.

A vertical file contains newspaper clippings, pamphlets, programs, reports from special departments and societies, on hundreds of civic, social and school subjects. This material furnishes definite information about ordinances, departmental organization and general city conditions. All statements are accompanied with references to sources.

Our periodical files give us advertisements of public contracts, county court calendar, building permits, new incorporations, conventions to be held in Newark, quotations of local securities, bankruptcies, sheriff's sales, real estate transfers and mortgages, excise licenses, automobile licenses and bank statements. We have ten real estate atlases covering Newark, New York and vicinity.

With this material we have gathered, as I have said, things of interest to men who are engaged in business of every kind. We collect business literature, finding its field, I am sorry to say, almost unexplored by any library agencies whatever.

We made quite a careful study of industrial Newark. We sent circular letters on the follow-up system to about 2,000 of the city's manufacturers. We were able, from these replies, to make quite a complete index to Newark's industries.

On the work of discovering and purchasing and arranging for use this municipal and general city improvement literature and this business material, the library spent a very considerable sum. The use made of it has amply justified the expenditure.

From the point of view of what one may call literary efficiency, it can be said that this kind of literature is much more effective than is the "literature of the student," so-called. I mean material on the outer margin of the field of belles-lettres, like volumes of comments on Dante or Shakespeare.

To explain further: If one speaks of "resources for students" in American libraries, you think at once of history, literature, philology, philosophy, art, archaeology, science and applied arts, and the mental picture is of long sets of proceedings of societies and of rare and ancient volumes. Slowly, with some reluctance, and only after vigorous suggestion, does one think of a "student" as one who is busied with yesterday's books and this morning's journals and the advance sheets of pamphlets not yet issued. As all admit that libraries should be helpful to students, and as students are not easily conceived of in terms of newspaper clippings and yesterday's journals and this morning's pamphlets and of directories of commerce and the trades, it is not strange that librarians have been slow in spending money and labor on these things.

Our civic and business material has been fairly well used. We feel sure it would be used more if it were more widely known. The trustees finally decided, at my suggestion, to try to promote knowledge of the things the library possesses which are especially useful to our citizens by the publication of a journal. As this journal was to appear in an industrial city, and as it was to exploit civic and industrial sources of information, it was decided to make it the opposite of academic—to devote its pages largely to civic and industrial news and the discussion of city problems. It was hoped that in this way it would win gradually a fairly wide range of readers, and those readers noting that their public library publishes a journal full of municipal and business news, would come to realize that the library possesses this kind of news—and then would be induced to use it.

It was not supposed that our journal, now fifteen months old, would make any notable contributions to the literature either of business or of city government. It continues, on the one hand, the kind of work already spoken of which led to the establishment of the course of study on Newark in the schools, and on the other hand, the kind of work that led to the accumulation of our large mass of Newark business information. Its basic purpose is always to advertise the library to the citizens. It is a new thing, quite new. The question of what information it shall give and what subjects it shall discuss is a difficult one, to be met afresh every month.

It has been, on the side of subscriptions, moderately successful only. The number of copies usually printed is 1,500. It has distributed 2,000, 3,000 and 6,500 on specific occasions.

One cannot say positively that it is doing the work that it was hoped it might do; but we believe that it is.

I notice a decidedly "literary" tendency among librarians, and a very natural tendency it is. When reference is made, in conversation or in public meetings, to the business side of life and the library's relation to it, some eager friend of culture usually goes through the appropriate incantations, calls up the ghosts of the classics, and, in their name, exhorts his fellows not to forget that, after all, the world is made good by doing good, and that the soul is more

209

than bread and butter, and the "the light that never was on sea or land" is more important than a good supply, at a fair price, of electric current.

1 have no particular objections to this method of justifying one's conservation, of making still more comfortable one's comfortable adjustment to things as they are. I will say, however, that I would be very sorry if I missed, in a discussion of this or of any similar presentation of the utilitarian work which awaits all librarians in public libraries, allusions to spirituality, vitality, culture, breadth, literature of power, and other things familiar to those who deal in flap-doodle.

MAKING THE LIBRARY A BUSINESS AID

Town Development, March, 1913

Do you know your own public library? If you do not, you should, and for this reason:

You are interested in the development of your own city, else you would not be reading a magazine called Town Development. Therefore you frequently want to get information about your city. You want to know, for example, why the streets are not kept cleaner. To help you to answer this question you want to know how much your city spends per year in cleaning its streets. You want to know how much this amounts to per square yard. You want to know whether the price per square yard your city pays each year for cleaning its streets is as much as, or more than or less than other cities pay whose streets are kept much cleaner than the streets of your city.

Again, you want to know why the paving of your main business thoroughfares is always in such poor condition; and so you want to know how the money spent in paving and repairs for streets in your city compares with the money spent on similar work in other cities.

You want to know why some of your school houses are built close to trolley lines, so that teachers and pupils lose about a fifth of all their school hours because they cannot hear one another talk. And you wonder if other cities do the same foolish and expensive thing. You want to know also about freight rates, rates of fire insurance, the number and cost per year of saloon licenses, and the city's sanitary condition, the prospects for improved sewage disposal, the character of your moving picture shows, and a score of other things, some of them connected with the welfare of your home and family, some having to do with the development of your business, and some being simply questions of general town improvement in which as a well-bred citizen you are deeply interested.

Now, you should know your own public library because it will supply you with answers to questions like those just suggested. Almost every public library in the country is eager to be of use in a practical, everyday way to the citizens of its community. If it has not the kind of information you are after, it would like to get it. In most cases it would have gotten that kind of information long ago, if it had been asked to do so.

It is difficult for a library to decide to spend time and money in getting information that would be useful to the business men of its community, to its active town-development citizens, unless it is quite sure that the time and money thus spent will not be wasted for lack of use.

You may say that your library should first get the information its citizens need for the better building of their private business and for the better understanding of public affairs, and then—should advertise widely what it has.

Well, that is what the Public Library of Newark has tried to do. It has perhaps gone farther than almost any other library in this work of gathering sources of civic and commercial information and putting that information where the city's active, commercial citizens can get it and advertising the fact that the information is in a convenient place and can be had for the asking. It probably has not done more in this line than most libraries would be quite willing to do, if they were asked. You should know your own library and ask it to help you and your fellow citizens in promoting your business and developing your city.

The main building of the Newark library is three-quarters of a mile from the city's center. The Newark business man does not need to go to the main building to get his information. He steps just around the corner from the city's traffic, commercial and office center to a branch called a business branch.

This branch is much more like a store than a library. It is on the sidewalk level, and has a big show window where books, maps, charts, globes, signs and pictures, often changed, make as interesting a display as does any show window in the street. Inside is one large room, with more floor space than many large towns have got in the Carnegie-built marble palaces which they stooped to ask for—3,100 square feet. The room is high, well lighted, quiet and inviting. It is open every week-day from 9 a.m. to 9 p.m.

Its resources include 13,000 books, maps of more than 1,000 cities, towns, states and countries of all parts of the world, 700 directories, which cover many thousand different towns and countries and scores of occupations; the latest publications of cities, counties and states on subjects of interest to Newark; and especially, of course, the official publications of Newark and New Jersey, ninety house organs, sixty trade union papers, ninety business periodicals, sixty municipal and local development journals; many volumes of statistics; a collection of the catalogues of 3,000 Newark manufacturers, very fully indexed; a good collection of modern fiction and of general

213

literature; and a special telephone service which connects it in an instant with the lending and reference center of the main library, or with its technical or school or art or fiction or order departments or with the central office; and—a messenger service through which it can get from the main library's collection of 180,000 volumes, in thirty minutes if need be, anything a patron calls for which the branch itself cannot supply.

A citizen steps into the business branch and makes it known that he wants the latest book on town planning, or shop management, or business organization or motor boats. When found, either here or at the main library, he asks if he can take it home. He is told that he need only sign a little slip of paper to identify him, and he can take home that book and a dozen others, if he wishes, and keep them for a month.

Then he says: "I am interested in some timber land in western Oregon; I'm going to send a man out there and want to know how he can reach it, what the country looks like and what towns are near by." The branch librarian offers him a 1913 calendar of Oregon with a full description of the county in Oregon in which his timber is situated. Down from the central library soon comes a United States government map of the region he asks about, showing it in great detail, being one of nearly 3,000 such maps on file at the library.

Then he says that he has recently invested in a brewery in southern New Jersey, and wants to see all the bills concerning the making and sale of malt liquors which have been introduced in the last few days into the State Legislature. The librarian hands him all the bills thus far introduced and seats him at a table to look them over.

Then he says that the great trunk sewer, which is to carry off the sewage of a dozen nearby cities, including Newark, is to go near his factory, so he has been told, and can he see an exact map of its route? The librarian hands him the last published report of the Passaic Valley Sewerage Commission with the route of the sewer plainly marked.

Being pleased with his success thus far and still having wants unsatisfied, he says he wishes a design for an emblem or a decoration of some kind, suitable for a letter head or a catalogue cover, one which shall suggest his business, which is that of making wheels for automobiles. Another 'phoned message to the main library's collection of 350,000 pictures, designs and photographs, brings soon a dozen designs, some in black and white and some in colors, in all of which a wheel forms part of the composition.

Almost every successful business man has a small collection of books, pamphlets and periodicals in his own office. This he makes use of and usually thinks that he has at hand information enough for all his purposes. He does not realize that he also possesses, in a public institution which he pays money to help maintain, another library, which he can easily use, very much larger and very much fuller in nearly all the kinds of information he needs than he has himself. This other library of his has gathered, or could gather if he asked it to do so, more information than most men of affairs have in their own offices, even on their own lines of business, or at least on certain aspects of it. Why does he not use this other library of his, as well as his own?

LIBRARIES

The fact is that few active Americans have ever learned how much help may lie for them in books and pamphlets and journals and maps and charts and diagrams, in the publications of societies and associations, in the directories of cities and towns, in the catalogues of manufacturing establishments. All this kind of material and much else the modern American public library is ready, as I have said, to purchase and classify and index if it but moved to do so by the demands for it.

If I may be a little personal for a moment I will explain that this business and civic service idea in public library work first came to me as worth while nearly twenty years ago, when I was managing a public library in Denver, Colorado. I found it not difficult to select and purchase such books and journals as would please school children, teachers, women's clubs, readers of history, biography, travel and literature and students of society, science and philosophy. I found it also not difficult to create such an atmosphere of general good will and public service and freedom of restraint in the library as to make it attractive to the kinds of readers I have mentioned.

But then I noted that the vast majority of business men in the community, men in stores, factories, insurance and real estate offices, and the like; owners, operators, managers, promoters, public officials, agents, contractors, builders, foremen, bench workers, mechanics, etc.—I noted that most of these men of affairs never used the library or called on it only for novels and an occasional book of history, travel and the like.

As I looked over the whole field of print, the whole output of the printing press, I became more and more strongly impressed with the vast extent of the accurate statistical and expert information, gathered at great expense of brains, diligence and money, and set down in print, which touches closely on all those activities which we may loosely designate as "business."

I noted, also, that very few even of the successful men of business, had more than a very slight knowledge of the great extent of this material, and that fewer still made any practical use of more than a minute fraction even of so much of it as directly illuminated their own special businesses.

I noted on the one hand, for example, that the young carpenter made little use of the educational opportunity that awaited him in books and journals on carpentry, building, architecture and design; on the other hand, that heads and managers in big commercial, manufacturing and financial concerns, cared little for the knowledge and suggestions of experts set forth in books and journals on their several callings.

To illustrate my point a little further; great manufacturing enterprises in this country have wasted vast sums in experiments and ventures which a careful study of the American and foreign literature of their subject would have told them to keep in their pocket books.

And again, right now in Newark, we are clipping from the daily United States Consular Reports, which every large producer and sales agent should have laid on his desk every morning, items that relate to Newark products, pasting them on postals and mailing them to local makers of those products, and—are surprising them with the information!

217

Truly, while libraries are thinking too little of being useful to business, the man of business is thinking too little of the things he can find in print in his library.

The result of my Denver cogitations was the decision that when the opportunity could be found, or made, I would try to open in a large city a business branch in that city's business center.

The opportunity came in Newark. We began in a very small room and did little more than stock it with the usual line of library books. As rapidly as the income of the library permitted we increased the stock of books and moved into larger rooms, until, about three years ago we secured our present place.

The "business" side of our work in the branch we were then able to push more seriously. Our purpose was to gather so much material, of the kind that can be useful to the active citizens of a large manufacturing and commercial city, that those citizens would feel almost compelled to use it, would feel that they were not running their institutions wisely if they did not use it.

In collecting this material we found great difficulties. We knew about what kind of printed material we wanted, but we did not know the names of the specific books, and we could not find any one who could tell us. We discovered here, that is, a field of print, the field of business literature, which no one had exploited and mapped, not even the librarians of the country who have done a very great deal in the past forty years to make easy the selection and purchase of books in most departments of knowledge.

We went on as best we could, searching out and buying and indexing, rather groping our way, and collecting gradually a unique and most useful mass of business information. We did not gather, and have not yet, more of this kind of information than some of our largest libraries have; but we seem to have been the first to put it together in handy form and set it down, with competent attendants, in the heart of a city's business district.

While gathering and arranging these business things we advertised them, widely. The use made of them increased. It has increased until we must either find larger quarters soon, or else devote all the space we now have exclusively to the "business" side of the work of this branch.

In trying to promote in the community the use of the community's utilitarian literature in this branch we were more and more impressed with the similarity between this kind of promotion or advertising and that of a commercial enterprise. We had noted the "house organs" published by many large firms, and the idea occurred to us that if the Newark library were to publish, in place of the lists of new books with literary notes and minor items of library news such as make up the bulletins of most libraries, a "house organ," devoted to Newark town improvement and to advertising the library's commercial and civic resources, we might gain the attention of the tax-payers and induce them to take more profits—by daily helpful use—from their free public library.

We did not start the Newarker to make money. It is a city's advertisement to itself of its own excellencies and opportunities, and especially of its own library's resources. It is growing in favor. If the business branch is as good a thing as we believe it to be, then its child and promoter, the Newarker will prove to be a good—as it is the first—public library house organ.

LIBRARIOLOGY

The Newarker, April, 1913

The greater part of this paper has been reprinted by the Syndicate Trading Company of New York for distribution by booksellers.

A daily paper, a nickel weekly and a 10-cent monthly—these make a library. It's a small one, yet it contains more reading than any "average man" in all Europe had in his house during the first fifteen centuries of the Christian era! But that is no reason why the average man of to-day should think such a collection is a good enough library for him and his family. In fact he does not. He buys a few books. It would pay him to buy more. Here are notes on how to practice successfully the pleasant art of getting one's own library.

1. BUY SOME BOOKS

Everyone should buy books. By that I mean that every person of intelligence, able to read ordinary print with some ease, will find that the habit of owning books and having them about him will give him more pleasure in the long run than any other habit he can form. Only a few buy and read books, to be sure; but then, only a few get out of life all the pleasure they are capable of getting. So the small number of the bookish does not prove anything except that the wise are always few!

2. BUT IF I DON'T READ?

But you may say you rarely read in books, and so why buy any?

Well, to this there are several answers. One is that books make fine furnishings. They do good to the room they stand in. They give your house an air and you are obliged to breathe that air! Then, too, they are tempting. Who knows when you will yield to the temptation to enjoy books if they are always at hand? And, again, there are family and friends; perhaps they will bless you for giving them a chance at pleasures which you miss yourself. And, again, buying books is a joyful task, and you cannot give your mind to it for ever so short a time each week or month, when you select the next volumes for your shelf, without getting a subtle pleasure much beyond that of choosing a new cravat or another picture or a new brand of cigars. And, once more, all book buyers are bookish, even if they never read in their books a single line. You meet followers of book fads, first editions, American history, sixteenth century poetry or what not, who will tell you they buy but do not read. Don't believe them. They may not read what they collect; but you may be sure they have their own private bookish tipples, in which they quietly indulge and out of which they get a mild but penetrating literary intoxication.

But here are reasons enough. The point is proven. It pays to buy books.

3. WHAT BOOKS SHALL I BUY?

Buy what you like. It's the same rule, you see, as the Great rule about Reading! Often one knows the kinds of books he likes, when he reads them; but does not know how to find more of that kind.

This trouble it is easy to get 'round by asking the public library. There you will say that you like this book and that and the other, and that you want to find more of the same kinds. The library makes a pretty good guess at what is wanted, and sets out for you a dozen or a score or a hundred volumes for you to taste and choose from; or sends them to your home for you to look over at your leisure. In this way you buy quite safely, and so do not cumber your shelves with books that are not in your line.

Or, you may say you want books of such a kind that, if you read them you will be posted on certain lines you are interested in. Here the library's task is easier. It can give you names, authors, publishers and prices of the best books on the subjects you have in mind, and can tell you quite accurately which are elementary, which are complete, which are accurate but dry, which are general but interesting, and, if the subject is one with two sides to it, which are the best books on each side. Then you buy what you think you need.

4. THE ABUNDANCE OF GOOD LISTS

If the library is not handy for a visit, then call it up on the 'phone or write a letter, and ask for lists. The library can show you, or lend to you if you call, or send to you if you write, lists of a hundred kinds. Some mention 50,000 volumes, arranged in groups on every subject under the sun, with notes of description and with prices. Others are shorter, down to a list of the ten latest books on the Panama Canal or on Producer Gas Engines, or the Social Life of the Egyptians 3,000 B.C., or on Paving, or Flying Machines or the Life of Richard Wagner. Some name the best picture books for children who haven't learned to read, or the best books for adventurous boys, or for lively girls or for the Young Man who hasn't Time to go to College, or for the reader of detective stories and of thrilling adventures, or what you will. Name the kind of list you want and the library can produce it—that is what it is for.

5. SHALL I BUY MANY BOOKS AT ONCE?

Sometimes, yes. Suppose you have moved into a good-sized house from the cramped quarters you have always lived in; suppose the children are coming to the reading age; suppose your business is a little less pressing and, in your evenings, you are a little less weary, why, then is the time to buy books by the yard. You know what are the subjects you want to read about, and so does your wife. Both of you know the kinds of novels you enjoy. Also you are sure you want the children to see on the shelves and to handle and look into and get acquainted with the good old books that they later hear intelligent people mention, that they will find mention of in their reading, and that they will be meeting in their studies as they go through school and college. In such a case the selection is easy, and to buy a thousand books in the first winter would not be extravagant or foolish.

6. SHALL I GET A BIG DICTIONARY?

When the time comes, yes. But first get books that you or your family or both like to read. If there are children about you will find they use dictionaries in school, and you will wish to keep ahead of them by having a pretty good dictionary at home. If the family has the habit of talking about words and their exact meaning and how to pronounce, get a dictionary, surely!

But you can begin with quite a small one. Some of the small ones are very good and vastly interesting to look into.

At the library you can see all the big ones and many of the small ones and can learn about others. Buy the kind that suits your needs. A big one is often just a burden to a man, in the way, and never used.

7. SHALL I BUY AN ENCYCLOPEDIA?

If you are the encyclopedia kind of a man, yes. And when the children begin to pass the ten-year mark you should have one for them to pull down and handle as they will. But it is easy to waste good book money on an encyclopedia. There are many kinds, and the best one for you is the one that, among those you can afford, you will use most. Some are for young people, some are for students. some are for average people with small incomes, some are for the rich. In thousands of homes are thousands of non-fitting encyclopedias taking up good shelf room that entertaining novels might much better occupy.

The library not only has good encyclopedias large and small, it also has much information on sizes, kinds, bindings, and cost; some of it found in carefully written books on the subject. Ask the library's advice before you buy.

8. SHALL I BUY "COMPLETE WORKS"?

No. Buy the books you want of any given author, and no more. You need not buy twenty volumes by one writer for the sake of getting the three that are all you care to read. The Complete Works Habit shows its effects on too many homes already. Rows of all that Brown, Jones, Robinson, Smith and other great authors ever wrote, not omitting what is worthless and including often his private and useless letters and a life by a commonplace friend—these glare through the glass doors of their cases in thousands of homes, and declare their unused uselessness by their bright and shiny look. In few homes are read the complete works of anybody.

Sometimes the best editions can be bought in sets only; but in most cases you can buy just the books you wish of any writer in just the style and price that suit your eyesight, taste and pocketbook.

9. WHAT SHALL I SAY TO BOOK AGENTS?

A very good rule is to say that you buy all your books at the stores. Another is to say that you don't talk book buying at home. Another, that you never buy on first look or half looks, and that if he will send to you the complete thing he has to sell and leave it with you for a week, you will give him a written decision. Another is that his book will soon be on sale, and much cheaper, second-hand in the bookstores. This is true of 90 per cent of the book agent's wares.

Another is that you buy only after taking advice. Then call up the public library on the 'phone and ask if the books offered are the books you need.

Traveling agents have persuaded many to buy books who would never have bought them otherwise, and in this way they have been rather helpful. But they almost never have anything that you cannot get cheaper at a store. Most of the things they offer are not what you really care for. Nearly all their "Fine Editions" are poor imitations of the real thing.

10. AH! THE SECOND-HAND BOOK STORE!

If you really want to decorate your home with some "Fine Looks Books," then go to a good second-hand book seller, like our own Charles Dressel, and there you will find scores of grandly beautiful "sets" which the "man who wants a glass case full of fine books in his parlor" bought through a persuasive traveling agent, and then in due course sold to our friend for a song as useless lumber.

At this same shop are also to be found good editions, sane, sensible, book-looking books in sets, of those authors whose complete works you feel you need.

The department stores have in recent years taken over the traveling agent's wares, especially since the recent disclosures as to the real value of some of the so-called *de luxe* books; and there you can find sets of every degree of excellence and at fair prices—often, indeed, at prices ridiculously low.

Treat the book agent kindly; wish him well in what is usually a perfectly proper business; but tell him you now buy your books at stores.

11. WHICH ARE THE BOOKS FOR ME?

You speak of choosing your friends. You mean that as you meet new people and come to know them you naturally pick out those who appeal to you, who don't bore you, who help you to pass a pleasant evening now and then, who have something new to say, who help you to see things differently and make life more entertaining. You don't pick these friends on sight, and you don't select them on somebody's recommendation. You get to know them first, and then hold to them if you like them.

Find your own books in the same way. The process is easier with books than it is with men and women. Of books you can get quite careful descriptions, from which you can often tell which of them you will like. Then it is much easier to examine a book than it is a possible new friend. The book is all there, in sight. The new and promising acquaintance may tomorrow show you a side of his nature that will make you wish never to see him again.

From the public library you can get a package of books sent to your home, books that you and the library have agreed may suit you. These you can look over at your leisure. If any prove to be of your kind, well and good. If not, you can try another lot.

You pick your friends out of those who live and work much as you do. You will find the books you want to read in much the same way.

Of course, novels take care of themselves. Poetry you want or you don't want, and for the present that ends it. Of essays you get enough in your daily paper's editorials. But if now you have not the book buying habit at all and think you may like to work into it on some special lines, where begin?

12. YOU WORK AT SOMETHING? BUY BOOKS ON THAT SOMETHING

Start in on your own business. Whatever it is it has an interesting history; there is romance connected with it somewhere, surely, and probably also art, and very likely politics and war and strange adventures.

For example, shoes. There are museums of shoes. There are histories of shoes and books about shoes and famous and learned cobblers and shoe-makers. All the long story of the invention and development of protection for the feet is full of curious, entertaining and amazing items.

And the literature to-day of leather and of all the other materials that go into shoes and of the machines that make them and of their distribution through the trade—of all this the literature includes hundreds of books of every conceivable kind, scientific, technical, commercial, biographical, historical. If you are in shoes, try a few of these books.

The same facts and the same suggestions apply to every calling.

13. From Daily Papers to House Books

You must read the daily papers; then you need to read a few magazines of the popular kind to get short stories of modern life and to keep up on inventions, discoveries and what not; then you must look over your own trade papers, one or two or even more —and there is still time left for buying and reading a few good books on your own calling.

Next, perhaps first, get some books useful in the house. Books on cooking, furniture, decoration, music, dress, entertainments, games, hygiene, and, if there are children, on their health and training, on their sports and pastimes—on all these and a score of other like subjects there are encyclopaedias large and small, handbooks, manuals, guides, compendiums, treatises and histories. Of these household books, many of them most entertaining and most of them helpful, how few are found in homes! Even of cook books the supply is usually limited! If in doubt, then, about how to fill your new book shelves begin with your own calling and go on to the every day demands of the house.

14. Branch Out and Take in the Two Americas

As for books on life and the world in general here are two good ways to begin:

First, sit down with this list and consider whether books on any of these subjects would interest you:

> Newark history.
> New Jersey history.
> New Jersey politics.
> New Jersey industries.
> New Jersey birds, insects, trees, shrubs, flowers, animals.

> New Jersey rocks, soils, minerals, mines.
> New Jersey farms and farming.
> New Jersey railroads, canals, water commerce.
> New Jersey roads.
> New Jersey maps.

In all of these and on the same subjects concerning the United States, you can find at the library books, documents, pamphlets and pictures, many of them published by the state or by the federal government and free for the asking.

Then look over this list:

> Our foreign trade.
> The Panama Canal.
> Mexico, Central America, Peru, Brazil; and the development and trade relations with our country of these and other South American countries.
> Canada, its growth and our trade with it.
> The far northwest and the wonderful development of Oregon and Washington.
> The Hudson, the Ohio, the Mississippi, the Columbia, the Great Lakes, the romance of their discovery and the wonders of their commerce.
> The story of wheat, of corn, of cotton and the rivalries of the world's great grain producing countries.
> The tariff.
> Our navy, our army.

On a thousand things like these, about which you find brief notes in the papers every day, the library has many books, some short, some long, some statistical, some narrative and fascinating. On any of these subjects, all of which come quite close to every man who works for what he gets, the library has books in abundance, and the best of them—or all of them—it will bring out for you to see; or it will take you to the shelves where they stand, or will send a dozen to your home for you to look over at your ease.

Some of them you will surely wish to own.

15. THEN TAKE IN THE WORLD

Go a little further with the list, if nothing so far named has seemed to appeal to you. Perhaps you say that your newspapers and magazines give you all you care to know on subjects like these. That may be true. But a trial of a book by a man who knows what he writes about, will convince you that after all most journals only touch the outside of things. They cannot pretend to do more. Their editors give you a little of many things and not much of any one, except local news.

> Flying machines, dirigible balloons, and submarines.
> Great fortunes, trusts and labor unions.
> Socialism, communism, anarchism.
> Painting, cubists, futurists, sculpture, art museums, architecture.
> The history of the alphabet, of writing, of printing.
> Printing today, its marvelous machines and how their product grows.
> How we think.
> The mind and the body.
> Materialism, pantheism, monotheism, pragmatism.
> Bergsonism, spiritism, monism, positivism.

LIBRARIES

> Education in Egypt, Greece, Rome, China.
> Public schools in America, England, Germany, France.
> The origin of language.
> What we mean by science.
> Astrology, necromancy, alchemy, chemistry.
> Myths, legends, fairy tales, superstitions.
> Fire, electricity, light, heat, power.

And these items are only the merest suggestion of the thousands of topics on which your library can furnish you many books and tell you of many others.

Take Egypt for example; you know something of its history, of the Nile and its dams, of the Pyramids, of its temples, tombs and sphinxes; of its English government and its recent growth. Leaving all these one side, here is a little book on what Egypt did for civilization, brief, fascinating, astonishing and reliable. They were doing great things in Egypt 6,000 years ago!

You can, under this first method of finding a starting point for book buying, either go over lists like those given above, or you can go over in your mind the topics you find in your daily and Sunday papers and jot down a few on which you think you may like to see a few of the best and latest books. Send this list to the library and later call and see what the people there can show you.

16. ANOTHER WAY OF FINDING YOUR BOOKS

Another way of finding your best book buying subjects: Get lists of some of the series of small books on all kinds of subjects that are now being published in England and America. Single volumes cost, bound, only 25 to 50 cents. The several series include books on hundreds of topics. There are "literary" books in plenty—novels, stories, poetry, plays, essays, letters, humor,—as well as brief histories, biographies and travels and good short books on science, religion, art, philosophy and society. Others are on subjects like these, each written by a man who knows:

A World Atlas (20 cents).
Evolution
Heredity.
Science of the Stars.
Hypnotism.
Bergson.
Synonyms.
Wellington and Waterloo.
The Nature of Mathematics.
Theosophy.
Syndicalism.
Cooperation.
Woman's Suffrage.
Principles of Electricity.

Look at these lists yourself, and pass them about in the home.

Some in the family are just now keen on boats, toy flying machines, tennis, football, wireless telegraphy, school hygiene, housing, photography, the stage, motor cars, gas engines, moving pictures, dress, rugs, laces. Won't they ask you to consider buying a book or two on their pet subjects?

17. THE FUNDAMENTAL FAMILY LIBRARY

Now you have a library. It is yours and your family's, and it fits you all like an old glove, because you have put into it what you wanted, and not what somebody said you ought to want. You have bought according to your own and your family's taste, education, calling and amusements. Your library contains the world's best books—for you; at least it does so as far as you have gone. Only prigs and pretenders will find fault with it, even if it has not one of the Old Masters you were tortured with in school days and have joyfully avoided ever since.

18. A POSSIBLE FAMILY LIBRARY

But perhaps you don't wish to plunge into book buying on your own ignorance and dissipate the ignorance by a touch of experience. Then all you need to do is to take the collection we call "First Aid to a Reading Family," which is all carefully described on another page, and proceed to buy it. As the descriptive note at the top of that list says, this is a very good lot of books. If you cannot or will not make your own selection, then this is what you need. It is not only made up of good books itself, it suggests other good books. It was planned to promote book owning as well as book reading. You and your family will use it, and, using it, will soon find it too small. It is not a complete library; complete libraries are most depressing. It was particularly planned to disclose its incompleteness. The books in it will demand more books at your hands.

19. HOW ABOUT THE GREAT CLASSICS?

Well, what about them? Have you read them? Have you read any of them? Did you like them? If you bought a hundred of them would you hurry home every night to read them?

You must answer these questions yourself. If you like them, then they are your books, and you bought them long ago. If you are very, very literary you have already read them whether you liked them or not. If you wish to know how some of the greatest of our fellow men looked at life, and how they described what they saw and felt and thought, then you must read some of the World's Greatest.

But don't forget that many of your greatest fellow men never wrote at all! They did things, and said nothing for publication. (It's the same way to-day!) And while it is true, probably, that the writing of great things in a great way is the greatest of all the things men have done, these greatest of all things —the World's Classics—may not enlighten you, may not give you joy, would only bore you—and—there is a very fine and delightful and amazing and absorbing lot of life awaiting you quite outside of the covers of the Truly Great.

Get your own Fundamental Family Library or our First Aid to a Reading Family and use it and see that what I have said is true.

20. ON THE OTHER HAND

A short plea, which could be made longer and stronger, for some acquaintance with the Great Old Books is worth adding.

A few of the old books were so well written or told of such interesting things or were so closely connected with popular mythologies and religions or with great leaders or reformers, or warriors, or adventurers, or with great national events, that they came to be read or talked about by many, and especially by those who wrote. Naturally those who wrote spoke of the beliefs, the superstitions, the events and the persons which are written of in these old books, and naturally also the later writers often quoted the very words themselves of these now familiar books.

They did this partly because they had nothing to say themselves, and could only say again what had been said better before; partly because they hoped that by quoting in this way from earlier books their readers would take them to be learned; partly because they wished by quotations to bolster up their own opinions; partly because they could make their points clearer by citing what they thought were familiar examples; and partly because they truly found the incidents and the things said in the earlier books to be interesting in themselves, genuinely human and wonderfully and universally true to life and very admirably told. Thus it came about that books of all kinds, save perhaps the dryest descriptive ones, are constantly referring to things in the Old Classics. Now, if you know enough about the old books to get the meaning of these countless references to them in the new ones, you, of course, understand the new ones better. Then, too, it seems to be true that we get very great pleasure from our recognition in reading, just as we do from recognitions of scenery, cities, friends and acquaintances; and if one recognizes and understands the allusions in old books and the quotations from them in what he reads, he gets much pleasure therefrom. As to the direct value to us of what the older writers said, that is another matter. That value is often greatly overestimated, and especially by writers who have no force or originality of their own and give us nothing but a useless dilution of quotation and reference from the writers they have absorbed, mixed with maudlin praise of them and artless prattle of their own.

Don't read books about great books. You were told about some of them and read some of them in school days. If you care for them now, read them, by all means. In any event put a few of them on your shelves for the children to see and read if they will.

21. BEAUTIFUL BOOKS

Beware of the agent with the very fine and very special books. They are usually neither fine nor special. In thousands of homes, where what is really needed and what was never bought, is the Fundamental Family Library, or our First Aid Collection, are rows of shiny, showy, begilded, neglected "sets," which cost ten times the money it would take to buy a real, live and daily used and greatly enjoyed and charmingly bethumbed lot of books.

A good rule in all book buying is this: if it looks "fine," don't buy it. Another, already given, is, if it comes in sets, don't buy it. And if it comes at the hands of an agent and is both fine and in a set, shun it.

There are beautiful books. It is not difficult to learn to know them when you see them. The library can show you quite a lot of them, and gladly will.

If you learn to know them when you see them, then you will take pleasure in them, and when you can do that, it is worth your while to buy one now and then.

Right after printing was invented 465 years ago, a few very beautiful books were printed. This was because the early printers naturally tried to produce with type and a press as beautiful work as centuries of practice had taught the copyists to make with the pen. They could afford to take plenty of time to the work, for if they printed only a few pages in a day, that was far more than the copyists could do.

But printing soon became common; then the printers had to compete for speed and quantity just

as they do now. The result was that after about
the year 1500 only a few very carefully printed and
very skillfully designed books were published until
quite recent years.

In this country to-day are being printed some of
the finest volumes ever seen. It would be worth
your while to look at a few of them. If you find
they give you pleasure, you should buy one or two,
or more if your purse permits. They are works of
art, just as are good paintings and good sculptures.

22. WHAT KIND OF A BOOKCASE?

The best is the plainest, of wood to suit the room,
not shiny, and without glass or curtains or filigrees
of any kind. Those in the stores are usually cheaper
than those made to order. But the store kind is
often too fancy.

The books should show; not the case. The nearer
the case comes to being invisible the better. Very
inexpensive cases can be made to order and stained
or painted to suit the room. Thus made they will
be not only modest and unobtrusive, not blatant and
glaring like most polished-oak-and-glass-door cases,
but also will fit the places in the room where you
wish them to stand.

In your new house, build no cases into the walls.
Thus made they are expensive, are usually not well
adapted to their purpose, and you are almost sure
to wish to change them within a few months and
find it impossible to do so without great expense.
Get a few books, then get a small case of the size to
fit a convenient space to hold them. When you need
it, get another case. Low cases all around a room
with a top shelf for bric-a-brac are sometimes good.
But usually a better plan is to get cases nearly

seven feet high, rather narrow and then put them just where they best fit.

23. SHALL I TAKE ANY JOURNALS?

You have answered the question yourself, for you buy and read from one to half a dozen newspapers every day, and they are in some respects the greatest of all journals.

Then of course you get one or two of your trade journals, you buy and take home an occasional popular monthly, and at home you find at least one of the journals for women. But these are not enough to give you and the family the pleasure you are all entitled to get from periodicals. This is the day of periodical publications. They cover every conceivable topic, and among them are many in which men and women who each know more about at least one subject than any one else, write about that subject. Of this kind of writing there is very little in our newspapers. The newspapers have not yet come to the point where they hire specialists to do their reporting. And specialists do not often write for the popular weeklies and monthlies.

Our newspapers get the news; our commercial papers do the same in their field; our technical journals are good; our journals of general knowledge of books, art, science, exploration, and general world-life are not what they should be in either number or quality.

Therefore, in the list of journals we have added to the "First Aid to the Reading Family" collection you will find several from England and one or two from France and Germany. They are very good. You need them; without them you cannot keep up with the world you live in.

LIBRARIES

First Aid to the Reading Family

This is the list of books and magazines spoken of in the preceding text. It is a very good lot of books. Put these books on your shelves and let the journals named come in every week or every month and you and your family can't help reading.

This is not the set of books you would pick out if you went to work to choose and buy for yourself. But, as the text expressly says, this collection is named for the average intelligent and busy man who wants to begin on a library of his own, but does not wish to take the time to do the picking and choosing himself.

Some will say that no one wishes to buy his library ready made; that each man is different from all others, and ought to buy the books that suit him. But while that is precisely what the text says, isn't it true that you buy a ready-made library every day when you buy your daily paper? If it is so important that you pick all your own and your family's reading, why don't you edit a newspaper for use in your own home?

Once more, these are good books, and will make a good beginning for the Model Incomplete and Always Growing Library you ought to have started long ago.

GENERAL BOOKS

Encyclopaedia of Etiquette. Holt. $2
Appleton's New Practical Cyclopedia. 6v. $18

World Almanac. $.25
Webster's home, school and office dictionary. $2.50

THE CITY AND THE CITIZENS

City Government in the United States. Goodnow. $1.25.
Socialism. Spargo. $1.50
New Worlds for Old. Wells. $1.50
The Spirit of Social Work. Devine. $1

How the Other Half Lives. Riis. $1.25
Efficient Democracy. Allen. $1.50
Changing America. Ross. $1.20
The Spirit of Youth and the City Streets. Addams. $1.25

LIBRARIOLOGY

MAKING AND SAVING MONEY

Every-day Business for Women. Wilbur. $1.25
Money and Banking. White. $1.80
Pay-day. Henderson. $1.50
Pin Money Suggestions. Babcock. $1

GARDENING AND NATURE

Our Native Trees. Keeler. $2
Principles of Vegetable Gardening. Bailey. $1.50
Wild Flowers. Parsons. $2
Nature Study and Life. Hodge. $1.50
Outlines of the Earth's History. Shaler. $1.75

GAMES, PASTIMES AND OCCUPATIONS

Model Aeroplanes. Collins. $1.20
Electrical Handicraft. St. John. $1
How to Judge of a Picture. Van Dyke. $.60
Wireless Telegraphy. St. John. $1
A B C of Motoring. Krausz. $1
Why My Photographs are Bad. Taylor. $1
Practical Bridge. Elwell. $1.50
Small Boat Sailing. Knight. $1.50
Book of Foot-ball. Camp. $2
The Wilderness Hunter. Roosevelt. $2.50
The Party Book. Fales. $2
Conjuring. Kunard. $2
The Book of Camping and Woodcraft. Kephart. $1.50
Boston Cooking School Cook Book. Farmer. $2
Boy Scouts of America. Thompson. $.50
The American Boy's Handy Book. Beard. $2

HISTORY AND TRAVEL

General History. Myers. $1.50
Short History of the English People. Green. $1.20
History of the United States. Channing. $1.40
"Boots and Saddles." Custer. $1.50
The Oregon Trail. Parkman. $1.50
The Balkan War. Gibbs. $1.20
Handbook of Alaska. Greely. $2
Russia in Europe Asia. Goodrich. $1.50
The Story of the Panama Canal. Gause. $1.50
A Tenderfoot with Peary. Borup. $2.10
Turkish Life in Town and Country. Garnett. $1.20
The Last of the Plainsmen. Grey. $1.50

STORIES FOR OLDER PEOPLE

The Street Called Straight. King. $1.35
The Red Button. Irwin. $1.30
The Magic Skin. Balzac. $.35
Buried Alive. Bennett. $1
The Rosary. Barclay. $1.35
The Mill on the Floss. Cross. $.35
Vanity Fair. Thackeray. $.35
The Talisman. Scott. $.35
Jane Eyre. Nicholls. $.35
Ben-Hur. Wallace. $.35
The Virginian. Wister. $.75
Scarlet Letter. Hawthorne. $.35
The Three Musketeers. Dumas. $.35
David Copperfield. Dickens. $.35

STORIES FOR YOUNGER PEOPLE

Two Years before the Mast. Dana. $.75
Robinson Crusoe. Defoe. $.75
Treasure Island. Stevenson. $.75
Tom Brown's School Days. Hughes. $.75
Last of the Mohicans. Cooper. $.60
Canoemates. Munroe. $1.25
The Lakerim Athletic Club. Hughes. $1.50
Swiss Family Robinson. Wyss. $.75
Fables. Aesop. $.88
Homeric Stories. Iliad and Odyssey. $1.25
The Adventures of Tom Sawyer. Clemens. $1.75
Ivanhoe. Scott. $.40
Hans Brinker; or, The Silver Skates. Dodge. $.75
Little Women. Alcott. $1.50
Arabian Nights. $.35
Fairy Tales from Hans Christian Andersen. $.35
Wonder Book: Tanglewood Tales. Hawthorne. $.35
The Age of Fable. Bulfinch. $.60

LIBRARIES

FOR THE PARENTS AND THE CHILDREN

The Care of the Body. Woodworth. $1.50
Telling Bible Stories. Houghton. $1.25
Talks on Teaching. Parker. $1
Education by Plays and Games. Johnson. $1.10
Red Letter Poems. $.50
Poetical Works. Whittier. $.50
Poetical Works. Longfellow. $.50
Pageant of English Poetry. Ed. Leonard. $.50
Poems of Tennyson. $.50
Tempest. Shakespeare. $.56
Macbeth. Shakespeare. $.56

The Children of the Future. Smith. $1
How to Make Baskets. White. $1
Children's Gardens. Miller. $1.20
How to Study. McMurry. $1.25

Merchant of Venice. Shakespeare. $.56
American Literature. Richardson. $.35
English Literature. Brooke. $.35
Sketch Book. Irving. $.75
Essays. Emerson. $1
Gentle Reader. Crothers. $1.25

MAGAZINES AND PAPERS

Life. New York, N. Y. $5
Collier's. New York, N. Y. $2.75
Saturday Evening Post. Philadelphia, Pa. $1.50
Ladies' Home Journal. Philadelphia, Pa. $1.50
The Sphere. London, England. $9
L'Illustration. Paris, France. $10

The National Geographic Magazine. Washington, D. C. $2.50
Popular Mechanics. Chicago, Ill. $1.50
Illustrirte Zeitung. Leipzig, Germany. $8
Die Kunst. Munich, Germany. $6

242

THE EVOLUTION OF THE SPECIAL LIBRARY

The Newarker, January, 1914

The character of libraries, their scope and the methods of managing them depend ultimately on the character and quantity of things intended to be read. When things to be read were written upon stone, whether in hieroglyphics or in sculptures or in ornaments of buildings, libraries were unknown. When things to be read were impressed upon bits of clay which were dried or baked, and preserved as records, collections of those records were made and kept, and libraries began. When things to be read were written upon paper or any of the many kinds of material which were used before paper was invented, it was clearly wise to collect them, store them safely and arrange them conveniently for use. Things to be read thus gathered and housed formed the first libraries properly so called.

After the invention of printing, things intended to be read became more common; but, as they were still quite rare and expensive, the old methods of collecting and preserving them were kept up and the habit of giving them a certain reverence was continued.

The reverence was due in part to the fact that few could either write or read, in part to the rarity of books, in part to the mystery attached by the ignorant to the art of reading; but chiefly to the fact that writing and reading and the practice of preserving books were largely confined to exponents of accepted religious cults.

As time went on and books increased in number and reading became more common, this reverence for the book decreased, but it decreased very slowly.

Books were for the promotion of culture. Culture was something which the upper classes only had a right to get. Science was pursued by few, and those few were scarcely admitted to the aristocracy of book-users. It is only within very recent years that in England, for example, the study of medicine and its allied subjects, even if carried on to most helpful results, gave him who followed it a good position in the social hierarchy.

The real books in the opinion of the educated among the upper classes, and, indeed, among all of the members of the upper classes who were competent to form opinions, were held to be, first, the literary masterpieces, the books which time had spared because they were thought to tell things so skilfully as to make them of interest and value to all men for all time. Among these were included all the older Greek and Latin writings, which were looked upon with a certain awe, largely because they were in Greek and Latin. Second, books on these classic books, studies expositions, criticisms. Third, books on religious subjects and especially on theology in all its phases and including philosophy. These books continued to form the greater part of libraries until within a few years.

When the public library movement took form and celerity in our country, about forty years ago, the accepted field of library book collection had widened to cover all kinds of writings. Novels were still looked on with a little disfavor, unless they were by writers time had tried and the ministry approved; science was closely looked at to see that it did not incline to infidelity; and discussions of sex and society and government were feared as tending to promote immorality and insurrection. On the whole, however, almost anything that had the form of a book could find a place in the public library of forty years ago, even though it might not be thought proper to admit it to the presence of a mere reader.

As a collection of all printed books the library had arrived; as a something established to gather all knowledge and all thought that the same might be freely used by all classes of the community, it had not.

The failure of the public library of forty years ago to address itself to all the community without distinction of wealth, social standing or education, and its failure, so far as it did so address itself, to find its advances welcomed and its advantages made use of, were due to two factors chiefly: the tendency of the librarian to think of his collections as rather for the learned than for the learner, and the tendency of the community at large to think of a collection of books as rather exclusively designed for those who had been reared to use them.

This long-continued, self-imposed opinion as to the proper limitations of the library-using group was broadened in due course for several reasons.

The output of print increased with great rapidity; and the newspapers, to speak of one form only of printed things caused a rapid growth in the reading habit and led millions to gain a superficial knowledge of many aspects of life and thought.

Public and private schools and colleges taught more subjects and taught them better, until finally the sciences were, a few years ago, admitted as proper fields of knowledge and tools of discipline even to the most conservative of English universities. From acquaintance with a wide range of required school reading it was but a step to the demand that a still wider range be furnished by the public library.

The habit of reading increased very rapidly among women. More of them became teachers, more of them entered industrial life, more of them joined study clubs, and these changes in their forms of activity all led to an increase of reading, to a wider range of reading and to a notable and insistent demand upon libraries that they furnish the books and journals on whatsoever subjects woman's broadening interests included.

Indeed, a certain almost apostolic devotion to the reading done by children and an enthusiastic welcoming of women as readers and students have been two of the most marked features in the development of the library work in the last twenty years.

Another change in library activities is now taking place, and is being mainly brought about by the increase in things printed, already alluded to. And here it may be well to refer to the opening statement, that the character of library management is dependent on the character and quantity of things to be read; and to call attention to the fact that the immediate causes of changes in the contents and administration of libraries—newspapers, children's wider reading, women's greater interest in world-knowledge —are themselves largely the results of the growth of print and the resulting increase in things to be read.

Modern invention, making printing much cheaper than formerly, has led inevitably to a tremendous growth in output. And by way of explanation of, though not as an excuse for, the failure of librarians as a class to realize the great changes in scope and method of library management, which the growth of printing and of the use of things printed will soon bring, it may be said that printing and print-using gained their present astounding rate of increase only within the past ten or fifteen years. Few yet realize that printing is only now, after 450 years of practice of the art, at the very earliest stages of its development and is but beginning to work on mankind its tremendous and incalculable effects.

The increase of print is marked in new book production; is far more marked in periodical literature; perhaps still more in the publications of public institutions and private associations; still more again in the field of advertising by poster, circular, picture and pamphlet; and perhaps most of all in the mere commercial wrapper.

Every added piece of print helps to add new or more facile and more eager readers to the grand total of print consumers. As commerce and industry have grown, print has increased also, and naturally and inevitably more rapidly than either.

Considered merely as an industry and measured by money invested and value of output, print seems to be growing now faster than any other of the great industries, among which it is one of the first; and in view of the fact that a like expenditure each year produces, thanks to invention and discovery, a greater output of things to be read, it must be admitted that in its products, properly measured, print to-day stands in the front rank of all our manufactures.

As modern production, commerce, transportation and finance have grown and become more complicated, they have found in print a tool which can be well used in the effort to master the mass of facts which daily threatens to overwhelm even the most skillful in their efforts at safe and profitable industrial management. In spite of all that is reported in print of things done, projects planned, tests made, results reached, in the ten thousand wide-ranging lines of the world's work—from a new gold reef of unexampled richness in the fastnesses of New Guinea's mountains, to the new use of a by-product of a city's garbage, much escapes, or, being printed, is unknown to him who can use it to his advantage. And so our worldy information goes on piling up; not all of it in print, but so much of it in print as to make that which is printed almost impossible of control.

The problem of efficient handling of worldly information is difficult enough in itself, but to this is added what we may call in contrast other-worldly information. Social questions which were seemingly quite few in number only a generation ago, have multiplied marvelously as modern industrialism and universal education have produced their inevitable result of complicating our social structure.

These social questions demand solution; societies to solve them straightway arise, and proceed to inquire, to study, to investigate, to experiment, and to publish results. These published results inevitably throw light on the daily routine of the industrialist, a routine already complex enough; also, they tend to modify public opinion or even almost to create a new and hitherto unheard of public opinion, and this new-born opinion again affects, and often most seriously, the industrialist's routine. Meanwhile this new social service spirit takes hold upon questions of government, complicates them, gives unexpected answers to them, reverses the old ones, and, so doing, affects in a startling way the attempts of the industrialist to establish and maintain his routine.

Of all this social-service and government activity the printed output is amazingly multitudinous.

THE SPECIAL LIBRARY

In any city of moderate size the social service institutions, including departments of the city, county, state and national government, and the private and quasi-public organizations which are attempting to modify opinions, customs, ordinances and laws directly or indirectly, through study, experiment, investigation, exhortation and demand, are so numerous, so active, so persistent and in the main so effective, and publish annually so many thousand pieces of things to be read, as to make it almost impossible for any organization to have in hand full knowledge of them all. Yet upon every enterprise in that city many of these countless institutions have already produced an effect, or will to-morrow, next week or next year. The wise industrialist would take them into account in planning his campaigns, and finds it extremely difficult to do so.

Add to this other-worldly literature the tremendous stream of worldly literature already alluded to, and include in the latter the vast flood of trade, technical and scientific journals, proceedings of societies and books and brochures from individuals; and then consider the difficulties which confront, on the one hand, the industrialist who would know of the social, economic, industrial, technical and scientific changes, advances and movements which may affect his enterprise; and confront, on the other hand, the organization, be it public or private, which is trying to keep him duly informed! Moreover, beyond all this is the vast field of research within which countless widely scattered workers, who for lack of swift interchange of knowledge of their respective successes and failures are wasting their time on misdirected and needless effort.

LIBRARIES

The change which this swift growth of things-intended-to-be read is to-day imposing on libraries can now be roughly outlined.

They may properly continue to serve the student, in the old sense of that word, the child and the inquiring woman; they must also serve the industrialist, the investigator or scientist and the social worker.

It is too soon to say in just what manner this new form of service will be rendered. The difference in the amount of material to be mastered makes a wise method of administration most difficult of discovery; and added to this great difference in amount is a difference in what one may call the proper length of life.

The technique of the management of printed material gathered by libraries has, in its development in the past forty years, been devoted almost solely to the accurate description, complete indexing and careful preservation of that material. So elaborate was the ritual in this field which was established and quite generally adopted some twenty years ago that to-day it costs a library of moderate size from 20 to 50 cents merely to prepare and put on the shelf each one of its collected items, be the same a pamphlet of four pages costing nothing or a scientific treatise of a thousand pages costing $10. And this takes no account of binding.

It would be useless to attempt here to describe or to enumerate the countless sources from which comes this mass of material which confronts us, and demands of the librarian a reasonable control. It comes from governmental bodies, public and quasi-public institutions and businesses; from private bodies, scientific, artistic, philosophic, educational, philanthropic, social; and from private individuals. It even includes print which is designed to advertise but informs as well; and in this line thousands of makers of things are putting out printed notes on optics, chemistry, travel, food, machines, machine products and a thousand other subjects, which often contain later and fuller and more accurate information than can be gained elsewhere.

Nearly all this vast flood of print, to the control of which libraries must now in some degree address themselves, is in pamphlet form, and, what seems to be of the utmost importance in considering the problem of how to handle it, nearly all of it is, as already noted, ephemeral. Herein; also as already said, is a characteristic which distinguishes it from nearly all the printed material with which librarians have heretofore busied themselves.

Everything intended to be read which comes into a library's possession must be preserved—such is the doctrine based on the old feeling of the sanctity of print which once was almost universally accepted. Even to this day those are to be found who urge the library of a small town to gather and preserve all they can lay hands on of all that is printed in or about that town. When President Eliot of Harvard a few years ago, seeing clearly, as can any whose eyes are open to the progress of printing, that print may overwhelm us if we do not master it, urged that great libraries be purged of dead things, the voice of the spirit of print worship of a hundred years ago was heard proclaiming that nothing that is printed, once gathered and indexed, can be spared. Whereas, did any large library attempt to gather, and set in order for use under the technique now followed, as large a proportion of all that is now printed, as it did of what was printed in 1800, it would bankrupt its community.

The amazing growth of the printing industry is overturning the old standards of value of things printed and the old methods of use, has indeed already done it, though few as yet realize that this is so.

To establish this fact is one of the primary purposes of the whole argument. To emphasize its truth, two more things may be mentioned, the moving picture film and the phonographic record. Historically these are as important as are any printed records of our time. Yet what library dare take upon itself the task of gathering and preserving and indexing them?

Here we have two kinds of records of contemporary life, both closely allied in character to printed things, which the all-inclusive library does not even attempt to gather, list and index. Difficult as it would be for any one library, or even any group of large libraries, to collect and preserve all these records of the human voice and of the visible activities of men, still more difficult would it be to gather and save all that is printed today.

The proper view of printed things is, that the stream thereof need not be anywhere completely stored behind the dykes and dams formed by the shelves of any library or of any group of libraries; but that from that stream as it rushes by expert observers should select what is pertinent each to his own constituency, to his own organization, to his own community, hold it as long as it continues to have value to those for whom he selects it, make it easily accessible by some simple process, and then let it go.

Both the expert and the student may rest assured

that the cheapness of the printing process of our day and the natural zeal and self-interest of inquirers, students, compilers, indexers and publishers, will see to it that nothing that is of permanent value, once put in print, is ever lost. Not only are there made in these days compilations and abstracts innumerable by private individuals for their own pleasure and profit; but also a very large and rapidly increasing number of societies are devoting large sums of money, high skill and tireless industry to gathering, abstracting and indexing records of human thought, research and industry in all their forms.

Select the best books, list them elaborately, save them forever—was the sum of the librarians' creed of yesterday. To-morrow it must be, select a few of the best books and keep them, as before, but also, select from the vast flood of print the things your constituency will find helpful, make them available with a minimum of expense, and discard them as soon as their usefulness is past.

This latter creed has been as yet adopted by very few practicing librarians. It is gaining followers, however, in the fields of research and industry whose leaders are rapidly and inevitably learning that only by having accessible all the records of experiment, exploration and discovery pertaining to their own enterprise, wherever made, can they hope to avoid mistakes, escape needless expenditures and make profitable advances in any department of science or in any kind of industrial or social work.

In recent years has arisen an organization called the Special Libraries Association. It came into being in this way:

A few large enterprises, private, public and quasi-public, discovered that it paid to employ a skilled person and ask him to devote all his time to gathering and arranging printed material out of which he could supply the leaders of the enterprise, on demand or at stated intervals, with the latest information on their work.

This librarian purchased periodicals, journals, proceedings of societies, leaflets, pamphlets, and books on the special field in which his employers were interested, studied them, indexed them, or tore or clipped from them pertinent material and filed it under proper headings, and then either held himself in readiness to guide managers, foremen and others directly to the latest information on any topics they might present, or compiled each week or each month a list of pertinent, classified references to the last words from all parts of the world on the fields covered by his organization's activities, and laid a copy of this list on the desk of every employe who could make good use of it.

Roughly described, this is the method of controlling the special information the world was offering them which perhaps not more than a score of progressive institutions had found it wise to adopt ¹ to five or six years ago.

At that time the public library of Newark was developing what it called a library for men of affairs, a business branch. This was in a rented store close to the business and transportation center of the city. The library's management believed that men and women who were engaged in manufacturing, commerce, transportation, finance, insurance, and allied activities could profitably make greater use than they had heretofore of information to be found in print. They were sure that this useful industrial information existed, for they knew that the most progressive among men of affairs in this country, and still more in Germany, found and made good use of it. Indeed they knew that they already had in the main library's collection much material which almost any industrial organization and almost any industrial worker could consult with profit. Such material was already used to a slight extent in the central building; but they believed that if what might be called "the printed material fundamental to a great manufacturing and commercial city" were so placed and so arranged that it could be easily consulted by men of business, the habit of using it would spread very rapidly.

From the first it was evident that the library was entering a field not yet greatly cultivated. There were no guides to selection of material; there were no precedents to serve as rules for handling it when found. Professional library literature did not help, because this particular form of library work had never been undertaken. It was not difficult to learn that the old rule, gather everything possible, index and save forever, must here be in the main, discarded, and the new rule, select, examine, use and discard be adopted.

But to put the new rule into practice was very difficult.

This question naturally rose, are others attempting work at all similar to this of ours? Inquiry soon brought to light a few librarians of private corporations, public service institutions and city and state governments which, as already noted, were also working on the new line. Correspondence and conference followed; an organization for mutual aid promised to be helpful and the Special Libraries Association was formed.

Merely as a matter of history, and chiefly because

the active and skillful workers who now have the
movement in hand, promise to make of this association an institution of very great importance, it may
be well to state here that the suggestion of an organization of those engaged in what may be called the
sheer utilitarian management of print, was made by
the Newark library, and that from that library and
from the library of the Merchants' Association of
New York, were sent out the invitations to a pre-
liminary conference at Bretton Woods, in July, 1909.

Representatives of about a dozen special libraries
were present, and the librarians of several public and
university libraries as well.

The name Special Libraries was chosen with some
hesitation, and rather in default of a better; but it
has seemed to fit the movement admirably. It may
be said, of course, that every library is in a measure
special, in its own field, and that state libraries,
libraries of colleges and universities, of medicine, law,
history, art and other subjects may be called special.
But a special library, and the special departments of
more general libraries—like the business branch in
Newark—are the first and as yet almost the only
print-administering institutions which professedly
recognize the change in library method that the vast
and swiftly mounting bulk of print is demanding;
realize how ephemeral, and at the same time how
exceedingly useful for the day and hour, is much of
the present output of things-intended-to-be-read, and
frankly adopt the new library creed as to print management, of careful selection, immediate use and
ready rejection when usefulness is past.

The story of the growth and work of this association of special libraries not only demonstrates the
truth of the statement that the modern printing press

is giving us a new view of its own importance and helpfulness, it also shows how rapidly the new view is being taken by the world of affairs; and, furthermore, it suggests some of the methods to which adoption of the new library creed is giving rise.

The association began with about thirty members, of whom more than half represented special libraries that could be properly so-called. In one year the number of special library representatives increased to more than 70, and in the next two years to 125. In January, 1910, the association began the publication of a monthly journal. The distribution of this journal, which has been very wisely and economically edited and published by Mr. John A. Lapp, legislative reference librarian of Indianapolis; the distribution of circular letters, reports and articles in the public press; the meetings of the association itself and of sub-divisions of it and outgrowths from it, all have served as an excellent and effective propaganda of the idea of the systematic use of print in the world of affairs.

A list of special libraries in this country, published in Special Libraries for April, 1910, not including libraries of law, medicine, history and theology and including very few public, scientific and reference libraries, gave 118 names.

Most of the libraries that have joined the association since its first year, 1909-10, have come into existence since that year. They now increase in number so rapidly that it is impossible to keep the record of them complete. One can only say that managers of scientific engineering, manufacturing, managerial, commercial, financial, insurance, advertising, social and other organizations, including states, cities, government commissions and the like, are, as the records of the Special Libraries Association show, coming every day in increasing numbers to the obvious conclusion, that it pays to employ an expert who shall be able, when equipped with proper apparatus, to give them from day to day news of the latest movements in their respective fields.

The journal, Special Libraries, has published a total of thirty-five numbers, over 400 pages, and has printed scores of helpful articles on such subjects as "The earning power of special libraries," "The value of the special library for the business man, the salesman or the shop expert," "Industrial libraries," "A reference library in a manufacturing plant," and many carefully prepared lists of books, magazine articles, new legislative enactments and the like, with titles like the following: Accounting, Motion pictures, Open shop, Short ballot, Efficiency, Public utility rates.

This association and this journal are described here thus fully because they seem to point so clearly to the coming change in general library method with which this whole argument concerns itself.

The fact that we now have an active movement for the establishment within large industrial enterprises of special departments for the proper control of all pertinent printed information, is of itself good evidence that the needs these departments supply are needs which public and college libraries of the conventional type are not supplying. Other evidence could be set forth from state libraries, municipal libraries and libraries of legislative research.

It is not suggested that libraries of the type of ten or even five years ago, public, proprietary, state, historical, could ever do the work which the enlightened industrialist of to-day asks of the special print-handling department he sets up in and for his own organization. But this seems evident enough from all that has been said, that the old type of library must modify itself in accordance with the new needs which the evolution of knowledge and the growth of print have created. Speaking of the free public library only—though what is true of this is true in a measure also of the college, university or historical library—it should try to master so much of the flood of print as is of importance to its community as a whole, and to those aspects of industrial life which are common to all men and women of affairs in its community.

This paper has failed of its main purpose if it has not shown that the public library should equip itself to handle a vast amount of ephemerally useful material, and should, by its methods in this work, suggest to the large business institutions how helpful they would find the adoption of similar work within their respective fields.

THE LEGITIMATE FIELD OF THE MUNICIPAL PUBLIC LIBRARY

Prepared for the International Meeting of Librarians at Oxford, England, August 31 to September 5, 1914

The question implied in the title set for this paper is this:

"What is the legitimate field of a free public library established and maintained by a city?"

To this question no answer can be given.

Social organisms—American and English cities for examples—are always changing in size and character. Their component units change through death, birth and immigration; and the knowledges, faiths, thoughts and habits of each component unit change within that unit's own lifetime. With this change in the organism goes, of course, a change in the institutions which the organism may set up, either to satisfy its positive needs, or to fulfill its wish to conform to certain customs found in other kindred organisms, or to favor a habit, like that of universal education, into which it may have fallen.

It follows, then, that a free public library established by a city, no matter how clearly defined may have been its character and the scope of its work in the minds of those who established it, will change that character and that scope as the city organism itself changes through the inevitable modification of its component units.

The legitimate field of work of a city's public library is, then, that field which the temper of that city may at any given time permit it, or encourage it, or compel it to occupy. As that temper changes, the field will change accordingly; narrowing and widening and using broad or intensive cultivation as days pass and knowledges, thoughts and feelings vary. The field actually occupied by a library on any given day can be roughly described—for that day. The field it will occupy to-morrow, and the field it ought to occupy to-morrow—this latter being what may be called its legitimate field—neither of these can be delimited.

I have thus tried to show that no answer can be given to the question implied in our title, not for the purpose of suggesting that discussion of the topic is futile, for I do not think it is; but to prepare the way for discussion. If we have no rules or principles which enable us to say that any given form of library activity is or is not proper, or legitimate, then we can look upon all forms of that activity with philosophic calm and consider their value from the rational point of view—that of pure expediency.

Of course it is not necessary to say that there may be found features of library work which courts of law pronounce illegal. These our discussion only remotely touches upon.

Let us then restate our question thus:

"What are some of the more interesting, recent and unusual kinds of library work, and do they seem expedient?"

Discussing this we keep within the range of opinion, and we arrive at tentative conclusions only. Discussion of this kind should be entertaining, at least; and, if touched with knowledge and some experience, and tempered by coolness, may be quite profitable.

I have before me as I write the last report of the Cleveland Public Library. The Cleveland Library was the first one of good size in our country, and I

262

guess in the whole world, to practice open access. This was more than twenty-five years ago. Since then, under the same librarian, it has taken up many new forms of library activity and given them full trial and pronounced them, for its purposes, expedient.

It carries on all the conventional activities of a library, such as buying and binding books and journals and lending them, and binding and rebinding books. On these no discussion arises.

It has recently added to its staff a library editor, who edits library publications, annotates books and promotes advertising. It is difficult to question the wisdom of this addition to the staff of a library which expends nearly $400,000 per year, outside of buildings, owns 300,000 volumes, has eleven large and fourteen small branches, employs about 400 persons, does much printing and advertising and lends for home use each year 2,700,000 volumes.

In the City Hall the library recently opened a branch which it calls a Municipal Reference Library. The name defines its functions, and to define its functions is almost a sufficient argument for its expediency. It has not been successful thus far. Few know it exists; few of those who hear it understand what it is for. Is this a good reason for withdrawing from this part of the library field? The librarian thinks not, and I agree with him. Many good institutions have helped to create the need they were established to fill. The librarian knows that most city officials, like nearly all men of affairs, have never learned how valuable a tool they have at hand in the printed page and in the precedents, experiences and statistics in the work of city management which may be drawn therefrom. He suggests closer cooperation with a City Bureau of Information and Publicity, already in existence, and more aggressive advertising methods.

A few cities have municipal libraries, independent of the public library. They are not all successful and some do little more than furnish salaries to incompetents. It seems clear that it is unwise for a city to maintain two independent institutions for carrying on the same work—that of gathering print and extracting from it that material which will help the city government to do better work. The public library has the plant and the experts; it can easily add to its municipal literature and engage more experts therein. A municipal branch of a public library seems quite expedient, wherever the need for it appears and the opportunity is given to establish it.

The Cleveland librarian speaks of advertising his municipal branch; and the question arises, how far may library advertising be wisely carried?

In Newark we have for three years spent about a thousand dollars per year, about eight-tenths of 1 per cent of our total outgo, on the publication of a monthly journal, the expenditure named being over and above the receipts. It carries no advertising. It declares itself as a publication intended "To introduce a city to itself and to its Public Library." This is an extreme case of library advertising. Perhaps none is more so. Is it wise?

The reasons for thinking that it is cannot be briefly and effectively stated. It takes up some of the cost of publishing catalogs and lists; it promotes the use of our business branch; each month it reaches and makes friends and patrons of a few men of affairs in a city where trade and manufacture are more definitely all-engaging than they are in most American cities; it promotes interest in our new museums

THE MUNICIPAL PUBLIC LIBRARY

of science, art and industry, offsprings of the library;
it helps arouse interest in the work of the City Planning Commission, of which the librarian is a member; it gives to the city itself a certain repute both
for the forwardness which it has, and for that to
which it aspires.

This journal, The Newarker—I send you copies
for your inspection and your criticism—costs less per
year than the wages of one good assistant. We feel
that thus far it has done more to promote the wise
use of print in Newark, to say nothing of its promotion of that knowledge of one's city which is an indispensable basis of and a powerful stimulant to all
proper local pride, than the best assistant could do
for us in the same period of time.

Many libraries publish bulletins. These are usually book-lists and little more. The Newarker
attempts to be in a very modest way an exponent of
civic improvement. It preaches a little; it expounds
much more; and it continually harps upon the fact—
though usually in very subdued tones—that there is
only one cure for poor municipal management—education; and that in the library are the essential tools
of education for any man in any calling—books.

The trustees do not ask, "Does it pay its way?"
but, "Is it worth the price?"

If the answer given them is the true one, then it is
evident that a library may wisely go far in spending
money and the time, thought and energy of its staff
in advertising.

Of the books bought by the Cleveland library last
year 12 per cent, 7,000 volumes, were in languages,
seventeen in number other than English. What of
the expediency of thus supplying to our newcomers
books in these several languages?

LIBRARIES

Our immigrants gather largely in cities and in groups by nationalities. They vote, they learn of the library, they ask for books in their native tongues, and their requests are granted. But that is a very one-sided statement of the grounds for the foreign language movement in American libraries. Though we wish to Americanize our immigrants, we also wish them to retain as long as possible an interest and pride in the countries from which they come. They adapt themselves almost too completely and too rapidly to our ways. A savor of their old habits and methods of thought would be a welcome addition to our national diet of industry. If the more intelligent among them wish to keep up with the literature of their homes, and to pass that interest on to their children—though this is almost impossible, as the children always insist on using English as far as possible—then to aid them, through our public libraries, seems expedient. It is easy to believe that they find their new home still more homelike, and become all the sooner attached to it, when they find one of its public institutions giving them a welcome in their native tongues.

How far is it wise to extend a library's work for children? It is not yet possible to answer the question.

Cleveland has perhaps gone farther in this direction than any other city. It has a director of children's work. In every large branch is a children's room, with a specially trained children's librarian in charge. It puts out "Home Libraries," chiefly for children's use. It forms and fosters children's "Library Leagues" and reading and social clubs. It has many story-hours. It opens libraries in school buildings. It lends libraries of children's books to teachers. Of all its books lent for home use 43 per cent are lent to young people.

To understand why a city offers such devotion to children's reading and general welfare through its public library, you must be quite familiar with our system of public education. This is no place to describe that system. It is easily the most prominent and most expensive of all departments of city governments. In my town our annual budget is nearly $8,000,000, of which about $2,500,000 goes to the schools. In Cleveland the total is nearly $10,000,000, of which the schools take $3,000,000.

I believe that while education gets as large a part as it should of the present total budget, the total should be far greater, and the schools, with certain other departments, should get far more. The annual cash outlay in Newark on motor vehicles and their upkeep, not including trucks, is about equal to the total annual receipts through taxes. In Cleveland the payments for motors are probably still greater in proportion. Where such conditions exist talk of the excessive cost of city management, and of its heavy burden on the taxpayer, is quite uncalled for, unless city money is wasted; and our cities are probably run rather more honestly than many of our big businesses.

I mention these things that you may see that, for the purposes of this paper at least, I find no harm in large library expenditures for children, *per se;* and that you may understand why the people of Cleveland look with approval and proper pride on the work their library does in this direction.

But, granting that Cleveland's expenditures for

children are legitimate, using that word in the sense
we have agreed on, are they wisely directed? I have
long thought that they are in some measure not.

The very fact that Cleveland's school budget is so
large, shows that it must have a huge educational
system at work for its young people. Many things
done by the library could be done more widely, more
intensively and more effectively by the schools.
Stories, pictures, bulletins, leagues, clubs, debates,
home visits—all these come more properly through
and by an institution with 85 huge buildings, 2,050
teachers and an expenditure of $3,000,000 per year
than from a sister institution of one-tenth its size.

Let me interrupt myself here to say, that I differ
thus frankly with Cleveland as to the expediency of
the extending so far its children's work, partly because I am trying to give you the beginnings of a
discussion, and partly because a quarter century's
whole-hearted admiration of the work of Cleveland's
library seems to permit a frank word or two of
criticism.

In spite of the large sums we spend for education
we do not get good teachers. I need not stop to tell
you why. Librarians think the schools—meaning the
teachers—do not properly train pupils in knowledge
of books, in their right use and in the habit of reading; consequently, librarians say, we should take over
as much of this work as we can, and show teachers
how it should be done.

That is a rough outline of the argument by which
libraries justify the wide extension of work with
children.

In reply it is suggested, that as the book-teaching
opportunity lies at the teacher's door; as she outnum-
bers teaching assistants in libraries a hundred times;

as she comes in personal contact with her pupils about a thousand hours in a year against ten to twenty for the teaching librarian; as experience shows that she can guide the reading and book-using habits of her pupils if and as she will, then the chilaren's work in a library should be, chiefly, not with children, but for children; not in guiding children, but in guiding teachers.

In my opinion librarians, as soon as they discovered the shortcomings of our schools in the matter of reading guidance, should have set about the task of correcting those shortcomings at their fountainhead, to wit, in universities, colleges, normal schools, high schools and with teachers themselves. This has not been systematically done. While this cries out to be done it seems a misdirection of energy to set a few young women, usually less well equipped in the pedagogic art than teachers themselves, at the hopeless task of supplying one all-pervading lack in a gigantic educational enterprise by direct contact with a minute percentage of the vast product of that same enterprise.

Libraries in our larger cities, and in many smaller ones as well, have built many very expensive branch buildings, usually with money given by one of the amazing products of our peculiar economic conditions. Concerning these, certain questions may be raised:

Are elaborate branches expedient?

Could branches be housed to greater advantage in school buildings?

Are the habits and feelings that work for progress awakened when our cities ask for, and accept as gifts from outsiders, certain costly additions to the mechanism they set up for their own betterment?

These queries may not be here discussed at any length; partly because such discussion would lead us too soon from our main topic, and partly because it would be too long.

This may perhaps be said:

The elaborate and costly library branch teaches by its mere presence, stirs civic pride in those who live near it, gives the library a certain dignity and importance which strengthens its hands for its proper work, and has, usually, such meeting rooms as enable it to act to some extent as a general civic and educational center for its immediate neighborhood.

But its elaborateness perhaps repels some who would most like to use the books it contains, and promotes the growth of the feeling that the institution it represents is, after all, not the community's own peculiar product, but a mere bit of bounty, of belated justice in the garb of charity.

It is now generally agreed that school buildings should be used continuously by their respective communities for, say, four thousand hours per year instead of for the one thousand they are now used. We are rapidly feeling our way to a knowledge of what should be the character of this use. It may soon appear that the schools can properly house library branches. If so, costly and elaborate library branch buildings will rarely be erected, and more efficient institutions than they could ever house will find homes within the same walls that hold that very much larger institution for social betterment of which the library is the hand-maiden—the public school.

The acceptance of gifts compels a certain complaisance toward the giver and his ways. This is an inevitable movement of the mind, and may easily

prove harmful. In the growth of municipal socialism, as marked by the rise, among other things, of
public schools and libraries, there lurks an abundance of dangers. These are surely accentuated by
an accompanying increase in willingness to accept
what one has not earned—not from one's fellow tax-
payers, but from an unrelated giver whose economic
manners, whether good or bad, we should be able to
look upon with perfect freedom and without the
squint inflicted by acceptance of his largess.

Cleveland has a very large collection of clippings,
leaflets and pamphlets alphabetized by subjects and
arranged in many thousand large envelopes. In
Newark we have a similar group of material, kept in a
vertical file cabinet. Ours is perhaps used more
largely than is Cleveland's to relieve us of some of
the terrific expense of cataloging. We put into it, at
a very small cost, thousands of items which, if treated
in the conventional way, would cost from 25 to 60
cents each to retain and index.

Both these groups lie outside, in large part, the
generally accepted field of library collections, in that
they cover the latest information, often quite inaccu-
rate, and the latest opinion, often quite crude, on
topics of interest chiefly to business men. As labor-
saving devices they may be important, and I am quite
sure they are; but merely as such they are not in
the field of this discussion. As tools for use in cater-
ing to the man of affairs, they may be discussed under
this query.

"Should the public library devote more than a
very small part of its income to an attempt to supply
local business with things in print of value to it?"

In Newark we answered the query with a yes
several years ago. We are still spending a good deal

of money in building up and administering what we call our business resources. Against this, perhaps the strongest argument is, that the traditional purpose of a library is to feed and protect the all-too-slender flame of the lamp of learning, to foster those more humane arts which have never too vigorous a growth; that just now all the training of our schools tends to look too directly to mere gainful ends; and that at least one field, that of the guardianship of books, should be tended with an eye single to the promotion of things of the heart and of the mind, and not of the pocket.

In answer, more can be said than can be here set down.

This at least may be noted, that the products of the press come forth in a mighty and steadily increasing stream; that of these products many are of immediate value to those who are at work at the very admirable task of making what man needs and what the present social order leads him, almost compels him, to long for; that it is impossible to divide our modern Amazon of print into that which plainly makes for culture and that which makes for better production and better distribution of products; that as all print comes to libraries, they must receive the mere sordidly helpful as well as the admittedly ennobling; and that it well becomes a librarian to put to its best use, within reasonable limits of cost, that which promises materially to profit his constituents in their daily task.

This may also be said, in passing, that to use the printed things of the day, even for the loftiest ends, and certainly for the profit of the man of affairs, the old methods of handling, by slow expensive cataloging, must be abandoned. We must arrange, use for a time, and then throw aside much of all that vast mass of print which the press now offers us. We must no longer attempt to catalog and store for all time more than a minute fraction of it.

Hence that encyclopedia of clippings in Cleveland and that elaborate and costly filing system which we in Newark call the most valuable ,of all our departments.

It may be said that any well-selected city library normally obtains and makes accessible all the print that the men of affairs in that city will care to use. To which I reply, that we think our business branch in Newark has demonstrated the contrary. It has been exploited enough elsewhere, and I can here say only that its strictly business features absorb only a small part of our annual outgo; its presence and use introduce the library to a part of the public which in most cities never meet book collections, and that very strong testimony to its usefulness and its rationality appears in the efforts made in other cities to establish institutions like it.

In most cities libraries use deposit stations, which are small collections of books placed on open shelves, usually in drug stores, with a small bonus to the owners of the stores on each book lent. These are moderately successful. But it is somewhat doubtful if this unsupervised distribution of books, chiefly recent popular novels, is worth the cost.

An extension of this same method leads to the traveling library, so-called, perhaps, because it travels from the library to its appointed place and back again in one package; whereas the deposit station books stay where put, save as they are changed in part from day to day or week to week, as borrowers may make requests.

LIBRARIES

Cleveland uses many traveling libraries; Newark has eleven. New York has carried the idea further than any other city. It sends books to 703 centers other than schools and recreation centers, lending by this means over 300,000 volumes per year.

Thus it reaches at comparatively small cost people in institutions who would otherwise be without the use of books, being inmates of hospitals or confined in prisons; advertises the library and the pleasures of books to people not of the reading habit; brings into connection with the library influential persons connected with many public institutions and with business enterprises.

Conversely, the use of these books has very little supervision by the library, this depending on the workers who assume the responsibility therefor, and may do it well or ill.

A library can promote interest in the fine and applied arts in its city. How far should it go in doing this? Most libraries go a very little way. They seem content, as to art, with their material enswathement of brick, stone and mortar, an enswathement usually of doubtful beauty and of manifest unfitness. Some venture on a bust, or a bronze, or a large photograph or two of accredited art objects, of a past so remote that in contemplating them criticism is quite lost in reverence. A good many have photograph collections, and here again time has usually made the selection and not the needs of the library's clientele. All libraries collect "art works." The phrase is commonly used to cover any very large and expensive volume with pictures in it. A book from the Vale press would by most be considered as unusual and be reverenced for its price; but would not be considered an "art work."

Four or five libraries have made collections of prints. That more have not done so is of course due to two things: the public does not care for them, and, as our schools and colleges do not mention them in their courses, librarians scarcely recognize them as art.

Now, are fine and applied art subjects in which libraries should concern themselves, save through the purchase and cataloging of books and journals thereon? No answer is forthcoming.

In Newark we have collected, partly by gift but chiefly by purchase, a few paintings, a good many bronzes, a great number of vases, and a group of prints so large that we may almost say that we have a print department. The paintings are not very good, and as in my opinion oil paintings occupy much too large a part of the art field in the minds of most, I am rather glad they are no better. Our bronzes are chiefly inexpensive copies of antique heads. Our vases are neither rare nor costly; but as rarity and cost have nothing to do with art or beauty, we feel at liberty to think them beautiful.

Our prints begin with the exquisite auto-lithographs of modern German artists—and some of these are on the walls of the main building and many of the branches—and go on through the products of all the processes and methods of reproducing pictures, and are accompanied by much material illustrative of the manner of print-production. This collection has cost a good deal of money and a great deal of time and thought. Few admire it or enjoy our other modest art objects. On first view they have not paid, and to procure them, has therefore not been expedient.

Nevertheless, I believe the attention given to them has lain within our legitimate field, and I am sure

275

that most libraries should give more heed to these same things. I do not say this because our modest art collections and the art exhibitions we have given in our lecture rooms have led to the establishment in Newark of museums of fine and applied art; but because it seems obvious that a library, gathering as it does the record of all the arts, should, in its minor adornments, use some of the very products themselves of some of those arts.

Moreover, *noblesse oblige,* we are granted by our positions a good opportunity to share as well as to tell, to suggest by actual object as well as to preach through the chosen page. Life is far too short, at best; but happily is easily lengthened by multiplying the interests of the day and of the emotions which the new interests arouse.

Large educational and decorative pictures— chiefly the lithographs issued by German publishers to illustrate history, geography—including maps— geology, botany, zoology, ethnology, anatomy, aspects of nature, architecture, painting and many other subjects cost from 30 cents to $1.50 each, unmounted. The library of Newark seems to be the only one that has spent time and money on the acquisition and lending of these pictures. We have about 1,500, mounted on heavy cardboard, bound in black, fitted with eyelets for hanging, classified and indexed and arranged like cards in a catalog for easy inspection. I send a pamphlet descriptive of them and of the manner of their use.

Each year we lend to teachers for school room use and to principals for school decoration about 1,400 from our collection.

Is this expedient? No definite answer is forthcoming. The time and money spent on them would

have added a few thousand books to our shelves. The
increase of the home use of books this addition would
have brought us would have been about 60 per cent
fiction. Would the increase in home use of books—
or in their reference use at the library—have been of
as much value to the city as has been the use made
of the pictures by and for our young people? I believe not. I am confident that in time the school
authorities will take over this work and carry it out
much more fully than the library ever can. Under
the peculiar conditions found in Newark—conditions
which I cannot here describe—this picture work
seems to promise certain advertising and educational
results of value to the whole community. Certain
of those results we feel we have attained.

Many libraries formerly spent much time in making picture bulletins. These were usually groups of
rather small pictures, gathered from many sources,
mounted on large cards and accompanied with rather
elaborate hand-lettering, intended to be beautiful
rather than legible, and all planned to arouse the
interest of children in certain books or certain groups
of books. These bulletins were exposed in children's
rooms, usually near the books to which they called
attention.

This work seemed to give more pleasure and profit
to the makers than to the beholders. It was not good
from the art point of view, and it had not a very
strong pedagogic basis.

The Newark picture collection is not in bulletin
form and the appeal it may make to teachers is only
one of the objects had in view in forming it. It is
an iconographic encyclopedia. It consists of more
than 50,000 pictures mounted singly, each on a separate card, 13x17½ inches in size, labeled on the card's

upper left corner, classified under 900 headings, and arranged alphabetically in a series of boxes, so adjusted that examination is as easy as the examination of a card catalog. In portfolios, also classified and labeled, arranged with and among the cards are about 300,000 more pictures, clipped and classified, but unmounted. Also there is always on hand a vast mass of material waiting to be clipped and arranged.

Many groups of mounts illustrate specific subjects, like the days of Queen Elizabeth and the nesting of birds.

These pictures are open to the public. As they include such subjects as design (3,000 items under 65 heads), architecture, lettering, portraits, sculpture and painting, they meet the needs of a wide range of inquirers. We lend for home use about 57,000 per year.

One must question the expediency of all this—and get no decisive answer to the question. Picture books for children are regarded as proper library purchases. Art works, full of pictures and quite expensive, are also proper acquisitions, for adults. From these pictures and books and art works, many of which we have cut up, mounted and placed in our collection, is an easy and quite logical step to an encyclopedia of pictures, covering pretty much every topic capable of being depicted, and adapted to both old and young. A book containing 350,000 illustrations, arranged by subjects under headings which serve as descriptive legends, cannot be found in the market. As it cannot be bought, is it not proper for a library to construct it?

We have gathered, arranged and indexed the names and some of the publications of about 1,500 of what may be called public-welfare organizations, non-profit-seeking societies but by no means all charit able, chiefly American. We found this material often furnished our readers with later information on many topics than we could gather for them from any other sources. It is included in the vertical file group already alluded to. Much of it is received as gifts, but the cost of securing it through correspondence is quite considerable, and to index it and arrange it properly demands a good deal of time of skilled persons. We have had no reason to question its value or the propriety of permitting it to absorb a small per cent of our annual outlay. Much of this material is ephemeral, being extremely useful today and becoming quite useless lumber in six months or a year. Our vertical file plan provides for a semi-automatic weeding out and casting aside of such of its contents as have passed their usefulness.

Mr. John A. Lapp, librarian of the State Library of Indiana, has recently been maintaining a bureau for the collection and distribution of information on public affairs. He covers particularly the field of legislation, state and municipal. A few public and other libraries paid $25.00 per year for the service his bureau rendered, which consisted of a weekly series of typed statements on the more important matters in the field covered. He did not furnish books or pamphlets, or indexes to either; but chiefly notes guiding us to the printed story of notable happenings in the very complex and rapidly changing world of state and city management.

This service is soon to be enlarged, and will cost four times the present price. To accept it is to cooperate with other libraries in an endeavor to secure, at moderate cost, so much of a view of public affairs in our country as will enable us to select from the whole field so much again, as promises to be of value to our own community. We believe, that although this work is quite remote from book-buying and book-lending, it is in fact a long step toward that kind of library management which new conditions are forcing upon us. All the world's activities are now put down in print; this gives us more print than we can gather and more than we could use even if we could gather it. We must now select and, of that which we select we must soon discard as useless the larger part. Co-operation in selection in one important field—this is what Mr. Lapp's work gives us.

Were this not in print I would not venture to send it, for it is far too long to be read to any audience. I have chosen a few things out of a vast field, hoping some of the things chosen may arouse an interesting discussion.

I regret that I was led to speak so fully of our own Newark activities. But, after all, they probably illustrate fairly well what is going on over here, and I can describe them more accurately than I can those of other libraries.

To refer to Cleveland once more, let me suggest that any who are interested in the wider field of the municipal library's activities would do well to get the last Cleveland report, and therein read of what American librarians consider legitimate activities wisely conducted.

WHAT NEXT?

Delivered before the New York Library Association, October 1, 1915

I wrote this paper, a short time ago, in the green hills of Vermont. When I found that I had to leave those green hills and spend a day in the woods of New York state, that I might read this paper to you, I was somewhat irritated. Perhaps the conditions led me to make this paper, not exactly irritating itself, and I hope not peevish, but slightly critical; not critical, however, of New York librarians, critical only of librarians in general.

While I was not feeling peevish toward New Yorkers when I wrote the paper I must admit that, with a Vermonter, there is always a tendency for irritation to arise when he comes into the presence of a New Yorker. You know the reason why. It is because of the scandalous treatment which the people of New York gave to the people of the Green Mountains 140 years ago. In those days Gov. Benning Wentworth, holding sway, as he claimed, over lands west of the Connecticut River, granted some of them to true men from Connecticut and Massachusetts.

These good men came north into the wilderness and took possession of their grants and set themselves to the arduous task of reclaiming and taming them.

Thereupon certain New Yorkers of detestable memory also laid claim to these New Hampshire grants and sent certain people across Lake Champlain to take possession thereof. The Vermonters, already on the ground, persuaded of the righteousness of the cause and the justice of their holdings, caught these intruding New Yorkers, tied them to trees, and im-

pressed on their backs the "beech seal," the instruments of application being rods cut from beech trees.
So irritated were the New Yorkers by the treatment
which they received at the hands of those best of
men, the boys of the Green Mountains, that when
Vermont, at the close of the Revolution, applied for
admission to the Union, as the fourteenth state, an
opposition was formed at Washington, largely oper-
ated by New Yorkers, which resulted in preventing
Vermont from becoming one of the United States.
The Vermonters, irritated in their turn, declared, by
the mouth of Ira Allen, brother of the famous Ethan,
that so long as such corruption ruled in the courts
of the federation of states they would withdraw into
the fastnesses of the mountains and submit themselves to the beasts of the woods and the justice of
Jehovah. And they did so. For thirteen years Vermont was an independent republic, owing allegiance
to none.

You can understand, now, why Vermonters are
sometimes irritated when they stand in the presence
of New Yorkers.

As the criticisms in this paper may be taken too
seriously, let me first read something which truly
expresses my own view of your excellences. Having
heard this you will understand that I am not seriously critical of the workings of your association:
"Both directly and indirectly, it has been and is today
a positive benefit to every library and every librarian
in the state. From the beginning it has stood
strongly for the best library ideas and policies, and
has been an effective force in having those ideas em-
bodied in the state's laws and practices. It has stood
always for the most liberal treatment of libraries by
legislators and local authorities and its recommenda-

tions have been influential factors in securing such treatment. It has been zealous in promoting high standards for library work. . . . Library training in normal schools, instruction in the use of books and libraries in public schools—ideas which are now being accepted in all the more progressive of these institutions, are ideas which had their first formal promulgation and recommendation in this state at a meeting of this association at Twilight Park, just nine years ago."

The war has shown us that we are quite uncivilized; are still able to act like dogs quarreling over a bone. Even in this country the war spirit is so prevalent as to show that our work with the "best books," our children's libraries, our classics, our stories and all our other well-meaning exertions have not abated and probably never will abate man's native ferocity. When Mars is talking books have to sit still. Librarians cannot prevent the breakdown of civilization! What, then, can they do?

I find no maxim suited to the occasion, unless it is "Let us be humble." And in the midst of our humility let us take a lesson from the English and find humor in our own doings and in the antics of our enemies—ignorance and sin.

But to invite you to a feast of humble pie is neither to prophesy nor to exhort; and you expect one or both. Do you not? What I seem to need first is a message, and I had hoped to find a message suited to the troubled times. I do not wish to preach business literature or maps or special libraries, though something on each of these may be expected. I wish to disappoint your expectations, of course.

In seeking for a bit of advice to give you which should be appropriate to a time of universal war, I said to myself, "Surely the jitney and the flying machine and the gas engine, their parent; the movie, the victrola, the submarine, the aeroplane, the type-caster, the offset press, and the war; to say nothing of telephone and wireless, have changed the foundations of human life, and the conditions thereof; and surely from a large view of these changes and of the revelations war has given us, should come a message, a definite program, for at least a part of our activities. But I seem unable to take the sufficiently large view.

Perhaps our work is so trivial that no industrial or social changes and no revelations of our moral state which the war tells us is very low, can afford any reasons for modifying it.

At present that is my own view. The library, like the school, is merely an unimportant by-product of a certain stage of invention, discovery and social arrangement. As a by-product it is amusing, to some degree entertaining and to a very slight degree distinctly useful. But it is so much a product and so small and insignificant a product and to so small a degree a factor that it can find, in the social and economic changes and hideous moral revelations of the time, no new doctrines for its guidance as a practical, efficient factor.

If I am not right in this present view then we ought among us all to be able to say something like this: "The movie is doing this and that to change our fellows; the gas engine is bringing the city to the country and *vice versa*; the offset press and the type-caster and the mechanical etcher are doing this and that; the flying machine promises this, the phonograph and victrola that, and the war shows that we are as black as we can paint ourselves and that solidarity of men and parliaments of nations are dreams;

therefore, we librarians should gird on the whole armor of our excellences and do"—— Well, what should we do?

Having shown that our work is so slight and that we are so much more results than we are causes that even world-changes give us no new moral codes and no new moral banners to lift on high, I am driven to repetition, to cast in new forms a few of our old maxims. To say, for example, that who sweeps a room in accordance with common sense makes both room and action fine, especially if he sprinkle the room with the fresh water of a kindly humor! Being unimportant let us be so smilingly. Let us exalt our calling for our own stimulation and make it so entertaining that our absence would be missed even though we have no speaking part.

I was first asked to speak to you about what the library of the future may be as a practical institution. I changed the title to "What next?" because, when I came to examine my topic, I found the reluctance with which I accepted your invitation was more than justified by my poverty of ideas. Not an absolute poverty, let me hasten to say, for the creative moments of our friend Bergson, when I feel that I am myself an original first cause, are not more rare than they ever were. My poverty of ideas disclosed itself as quite complete when, as my opening remarks have told you, I asked myself this question: "Our fellow men having proved themselves fundamentally uncivilized, in spite of twenty-five or thirty centuries of books, five centuries of printers and forty years of zealous and mission-hearted American librarians, what should the said American librarians do?"

Do you say that we should go on putting the right book in the right hands at the right moment? And will that persuade any not to fight, or to make shells, or to sell munitions or—except Mr. Rockefeller—to lend money to those who are fighting? Some have said to me that it were better for mankind if in my own library work I put less emphasis on industry and more on culture and uplift; less on mere books and more on books of power; less on directories and more on Walter Pater and Henry Van Dyke. And I must reply by saying that the nations that have most freely wallowed for several centuries in "books of power" are the ones which are now wading deepest in one another's blood!

I am perfectly well aware that you do not think I am giving you the practical talk to which you are entitled. But I think I am. The first thing to do when you are going to build is to survey the site. The site for the practical—and the word as it was given to me, of course, meant useful—for the useful library edifice we hope to build is right in the center of poor human nature, and this center is now a morass of greed, servility, prejudice, national hatred and general beastliness, as Europe demonstrates. Surely it is an entirely practical proceeding first to look frankly at this morass and learn, if we can, if libraries will help a little in its drainage and puri- fication, before we draw our plans and certainly before we venture to gaze with holy joy on the mere mirage of a noble and useful structure born of the heat of a baseless enthusiasm!

Now, if you will grant that the spirit which makes wars is so firmly rooted in us by the thousands of years of fighting through which man came to be what he is that it cannot be eradicated save by centuries of effort; and if you will grant that you cannot properly today treat of the future of the library as a useful thing without first of all examining its possible activities in the light of a frightful war; and if you grant that as an institution for ending war it is quite negligible, even if it heroically holds to red ink on its catalog cards, and stands solidly for the ribbon arrangement of fiction, and refuses to buy any more of Mr. Chambers' novels—then I will leave the subject and return to fault-finding, advice and prognosis.

Librarians are continually coming together to hear the talk of persons who have never written great books. That is a strange performance for persons whose mission in life it is to induce people to read the best books, is it not? I suppose it is true that those who cannot read must listen, or die in ignorance. But librarians can surely gather an ample supply of sweetness and riches from the printed page. Indeed, they are so skilled in this art, and have so great a faith in it, that they preach countless sermons on it. But, if librarians can read to profit, why do they so often meet to listen? They call the young away from the talker on the street, they rush books into a village to divert the participants from their local academy of the country store, they preach reading early and late, and write hymns to the printed page, and burn incense before the bound volume; and then they run off to a meeting to hear somebody say a little something that has been better said in print, if it was ever worth saying at all!

Oh! of course, there is the interchange of spirit at the meeting; the magic of together, and the informal discussions where we learn so much, and the inspirational atmosphere—of this paper, for example! But, first, if those are the things for which library meetings exist, why not omit the talks? And, second, according to the missionary literature of our sect, there is nothing so uplifting, so humanizing and even so informing as books. Really and truly, now, can you deny that books are nobler, more masterly, more spiritual, more inspirational, more vitally social than any talk at any inn even by an intelligent librarian and still more intelligent laymen?

I will now turn about and admit that there are certain good things which can be accomplished only through meetings like this. But I am quite sure that there are too many of these meetings. And I am sure, also, that you ought to bring to your meetings much more of definite, careful work; I mean the clearly stated results of hard work of the previous year. This work is waiting to be done. Then these results should be printed and made available to the library world.

Is that what you call a practical suggestion? Do you admit that the library as a practical institution would be much more influential if you all accepted your own primal and oft repeated doctrine and read and studied each year more of those good books you are pressing upon others; if you then formulated the conclusions of your reading and your study, and compared notes with one another; and if you then, at occasional meetings like this, brought out your conclusions to be tested; and if, finally, having found that a promising residuum is left, gave it to the world?

I have for long years preached and written on this practical suggestion; but the preaching and the writing have not persuaded you, and, not at all to my surprise, you persist in your intemperance in listening. Though avowed protagonists of the practice of reading, in your hearts you are worshippers of preachers. You pray for more eye-mindedness in the world; but are yourselves ear-minded. You are not ashamed to feel that you are exercising and strengthening your intellects at meetings like this, when you are, in fact, merely gratifying your auditory centers with the cadences of a tinkling voice. Ignorant nonreaders, of whom the world is full, must be permitted to listen much. They must even be permitted to think that they have greatly developed their intellects when they have once heard a man of note declaim. But, for us, who are readers and preachers of reading, these delights and satisfactions in listening ought to be rare and greatly restrained.

It was plain to me that in the title suggested for my talk—"the future of the library as a practical institution"—the word practical meant useful, breadwinning, business-promoting. I was to speak on the business man and of the sweet influence on him of the last New Zealand year book and of the post route map of Arkansas; and I was to show that the library of the future—not forgetting the things of the spirit, oh no, by no means! and not neglecting uplift, and not failing to pass a kind word to inspiration as I went along—I was to show that the library of the future will surely soon take its place as a useful and important factor in the world of affairs. Well, in my opinion, I do not need to prove to you that libraries are going to be far more useful, far more practical, far more closely allied to industrialism than they have ever been. Their advance in this direction is, right now, very rapid, and so open to the observant eye that any librarian who does not see it may be sure that his or her library is not of the kind which most of the libraries in the country soon will be.

In time the library is going to be of great importance in the world; but this importance will not be very fully shared in by libraries of the present prevailing type. We shall be obliged to change our scope and methods a good deal if we are to become usefully important or importantly useful.

You see, what the book does, it does quietly. Even in education the results of its work are not obvious. One boy studies books and his brain develops; but father and old Vox Populi cannot see his brain, and cannot realize that his work on books is producing results. Another boy hammers a piece of perfectly good copper into something as ugly as sin, and this the father and Vox Populi can see at once is a result, a product, and they admire, and wonder, and say, "Behold what practical training can do for a boy!"

And thereupon cities and universities proceed to spend millions on equipment for practical training, and a few begrudged hundreds on books with, perhaps, for the university, a preposterous monument thrown in to fill the eye and store the few books.

The silence of the book and the invisibility of its handiwork, these are two of our great handicaps, not to be overcome either by talking ourselves or by listening to great speakers. In spite of them, however, it is perfectly obvious that the book—and the book in the new library nomenclature means print in any form—will soon be an important factor in every bit of the world's handwork. In time we shall become those veritable print-using animals which we librarians have long praised as the highest of created beings.

Here I wish to pause and tell you about three things with which I have come in touch in recent months and which perhaps give point to the facts on which my suggestion is based: to wit, the prodigious change in the print-producing and the print-using habits that has recently come upon us, and the accompanying changes that should be made in library administration.

It has been my pleasure, this summer, to have a hand in the beautification of, and the work of, the county fair at Woodstock, Vermont. Among the other things which the committee I was connected with carried on, was this: They sent, at my suggestion, to about 150 state institutions and social service organizations having to do with any aspect of rural life, a circular letter asking these organizations each to send to the county fair a supply of the pamphlet literature they issue; there to be distributed. As the result of these letters we had, at the county fair, many copies of each of a thousand different pamphlets on farm life. They covered farming in general, fertilizing, fence-making, care of stock, raising chickens, hygiene in the home, care of infants and many other topics. It is not too much to say that, if these pamphlets had been printed in a little different form, after the manner of the conventional book, they would have formed a library of a thousand volumes of the best and latest literature on the farm and farm life. These books, or pamphlets, were displayed on shelves by kinds and distributed to all comers. So much of the literature as was not taken on these two days will be distributed by the local superintendent of schools. This is library work of a new kind.

One of the most interesting and intricate of all modern callings is that of the credit man—the man who decides for a business house to whom credit shall be given, and for how much, and under what circumstances. To do this work wisely he must know his United States well, the character of the population in the different centers, and the character and possibilities of the industries here and there. These credit men have learned that the printed page is, above all other things, the most valuable tool they can use in acquiring the information they need. The local association in Newark has asked us to prepare a list of the best books for the use of credit men, in equipping themselves for work, and have said that they wish this list made as good as possible and that they will pay the cost of publishing the same, regardless of its length. This, again, is, perhaps, library work of a new kind.

The Associated Advertising Clubs of the World is one of the most powerful organizations of its kind. Among the many activities of this organization is the establishment of collections of books for the use of advertising men, either independent libraries or departments in public libraries. I have the good fortune to be the chairman of a Committee on Libraries under the direction of the General Committee on Education of this organization and hope to be able, through this position, to be of assistance in promoting the acceptance by public libraries of the doctrine that library management must, in some respects, be notably modified to meet changing conditions in the use of print.

And here comes my practical suggestion which, as I hope you will see, draws together and makes fairly logical all that I have been saying. The suggestion is based on the fact that by far the greater part of all print today is outside the field of the conventional library; and on the further fact, partly a result of the first, that the library of to-day is not a very important factor in human life.

The suggestion is that you appoint a committee or

WHAT NEXT?

a group of committees to examine into and report upon the use of print to-day and the relation of the present prevailing type of public library to that use.

The printing press is pouring out a mighty stream of print. This stream is helping to turn the wheels of the machine shops of human activity. Conventional public libraries seem as tiny skiffs on this stream, and their occupants as almost solely concerned with the navigation of their respective skiffs. Or, if you prefer the figure, these libraries are as backwaters and eddies, turning flotsam and jetsam slowly round and round, with bits of treasure trove scattered here and there through the mass.

In any event, and regardless of figures good or bad, my advice is that you discover where libraries are to-day, what relation they bear to the world's use of print, and then discover, if you can, how that relation can be made one of indispensable utility.

INDEX

INDEX

INDEX

Indexes to society and scientific publications, Burden of, 64
Iles, George, 37, 65, 80
Information desk, location, 26
Information or vertical file, 207, 271

Kennedy, J. W., Course of study on the city of Newark, 205

Legitimate field of the municipal public library, 261
Lending department, plan and location, 26
Librarian, a worker, 8
Librarian, an office-holder, 187
Librarian's enthusiasm, 39
Librarian's influence, 13, 121
Librarians' meetings, 287
Librarianship, a public business, 189
Librarianship as a profession, 9, 39, 41, 171, 189, 209
Libraries, Increase in number and growth of, 79
Libraries, Origin of, 243
Librariology, 130, 221
Library associations, state and local, 123
Library construction, some general principles, 22, 54, 63
Library, Course of instruction in the use of, 197
Library meetings, Faults of, 129
Library methods, Changes in, 53, 55, 63, 65, 148, 206
Library organizations, How to form, 126
Library, relation to the community, 12, 41, 71, 136, 178
Library, Work of, for county fair, 291
Library's functions, 15, 51, 60, 66, 69, 73, 135, 153, 261
Light rooms in library buildings, Necessity for, 23
Literary criticism not reliable, 36
Literary journals, Book reviews in, 34

Made-in-Newark index 200
Magazines for private library, 242
Management of modern public libraries, 16, 19
Management problems, 250
Map collection, 206
Meetings in library buildings, 71, 118
Model home library, List of books for, 240
Municipal affairs, publicity and the public library, 203, 212
Municipal improvement organizations and the public library, 72
Municipal information, Collection of, 205
Municipal league library, 190
Municipal libraries, 191, 264
Municipal public library, its legitimate field, 261
Municipal reference library, Cleveland, 263
Museums, Need of, 73, 199

National Educational Association, library department, 11
Natural history stories for children, 108
Naudé on the management of libraries, 51
Newark business branch library, 200, 206, 213, 217, 254
Newark, check list of organizations, 132
Newark, course of study, 196, 205
Newark library building, Use of, for meetings 195
Newark library, Notes about, 191, 198
Newark Museum Association organization, 199
Newark newspaper items about library, 117
Newarker, The, 200, 208, 219, 264
Newspapers, Publicity for library through, 85, 115, 139
Newspapers, analysis of contents, 46
Newspapers and periodicals, Instruction in use of, needed, 49

INDEX

INDEX